Cycle Touring in Germany
A selection of notes

Peter Adcock

**Copyright © 2020 Peter Adcock
All rights reserved.**

First version - April 2020

"It is the unknown around the corner that turns my wheels" — *Heinz Stücke, German long-distance touring cyclist*

Introduction

Once a year I go away for a week or so cycle touring, usually in Europe with four others (we met whilst working for a life and pensions company in Bristol in the late 1980s). Each trip has been different and memorable for many reasons.

Up to 2011, we had mainly been to northern France (apart for a few days in Guernsey) i.e. places we could get to easily from Le Havre or Caen via ferry from Portsmouth and various trains to (for instance) Rouen or Fecamps to get us away from the coast. In 2011 we broke with tradition and didn't go to northern France but went further afield to Germany.

We now had the bug to go further afield and for longer.

As we are not getting any younger and are beginning to forget things, we decided to write some notes. They've languished on various hard drives for a few years so we decided that maybe it's time we shared them with a wider audience.

These notes are very much a joint effort but as we were accumulating a few after a number of trips, I volunteered to pull them together and add more information, remove personal information (and the odd swear word) make them more consistent in look and feel and make them available should they be useful for anyone else considering a similar trip.

We have notes for trips to both France and Germany which have all been published separately as e-books. This is an attempt to pull them all together into a larger volume, one for each country. This is the German volume and comprises:

- 2011; Cycling the Elbe Cycle Route (*Elberadweg*)

- 2013; Cycling the Black Forest Cycle Way (Südschwarzwald-Radweg)

- 2018; Cycling the Weser-Radweg - Hann. Münden to Minden

How did it all start?

I'd done a couple of cycling trips to France in the 1970s and always wanted to go back for more. It's a shame it took 30 years to actually do it! It was fairly easy for me, I was brought up in Southampton and at that time, it was possible to catch a ferry from Southampton to northern France. This eventually ended after all cross channel ferry services moved to Portsmouth with a brief attempt to resurrect it in the 1990s.

Along with many of my friends we had summer jobs in Southampton so it was easy to leave work, cycle to the docks, get on a ferry, spend a couple of days cycling around, another overnight ferry back and straight to work! Not sure I could do that now!

***

Our first trip as a group was from Thursday 19th August to Sunday 22nd August 2004 to Le Havre. Planning was minimal apart from booking ferry tickets and taking tents.

Recently some very high level notes have come to light, a brief summary of what you can do with a bike, tent, ferry tickets and optimism!

Cycling the Elbe Cycle Route
(*Elberadweg*)
Lutherstadt Wittenberg to the Czech border

"Cyclers see considerable more of this beautiful world than any other class of citizens. A good bicycle, well applied, will cure most ills this flesh is heir to" - Dr. K. K. Doty

Introduction

We decided we needed to start travelling further afield, this trip was a departure from previous years in many ways, a first trip to Germany, a flight rather than a ferry and also the one and only time (to date) we've taken bikes (as a group) on a plane.

What were we about to attempt?

The Elbe Cycle Route (*Elberadweg* in German) is part of an international network of cycling routes all over Europe. It is one of nearly 40 integrated river cycling routes in Germany and by far the most popular route for cyclists in that country.

The Elbe Cycle Route starts in Špindlerův Mlýn in the Krkonoše mountains. It then runs for about 1,220km until Cuxhaven on the North Sea coast. Part of it runs together with EuroVelo 7 (EV7), part of the extensive EuroVelo network. EV7, named the *Sun Route*, is a 7,409km EuroVelo long-distance cycling route running north–south through the whole of Europe from the North Cape in Norway to the island of Malta in the Mediterranean Sea. The route passes through nine countries and from north to south these are: Norway, Finland, Sweden, Denmark, Germany, Czech Republic, Austria, Italy, Malta.

After the Czech part of the route, it runs through the Elbe Sandstone Mountains crossing the border to Germany. Shortly after this the route runs through Dresden then other cities such as Meißen, Lutherstadt Wittenberg, Dessau, Magdeburg, Tangermünde, Lauenburg, Hamburg and Cuxhaven.

One of the other reasons for its popularity is probably the fact that there are no significant level changes from Dresden on. It is practically downhill all the way from Dresden north to Cuxhaven but can be into a slight headwind if attempted in that direction.

The Elbe Cycling Route is clearly marked throughout Germany with its sign; a stylised "e" with Elbe*rad*weg written underneath. It is also possible to follow the EV 7 sign which is the EU flag and a number 7 in the middle. There are also many local signs for cyclists clearly showing the route and distances between places.

On previous (and many subsequent) trips we've camped. This time we decided to stay at small hotels and B & Bs. This was because there weren't a huge number of campsites in this area and there's little point in taking camping stuff for just one or two nights. Not camping meant we could take less stuff i.e. no tent, sleeping bag or sleeping mat.

We didn't attempt the entire route! This is an account of part of it cycling south from Lutherstadt Wittenberg to just across the Czech border south of Bad Schandau. At least it should give the reader a flavour of the trip and maybe inspire you to attempt something similar.

Thursday 1st September - Bristol - Berlin Schönefeld

Taking bikes on a plane is not as problematic as you might think and well worth considering if you want to use your own bike rather than hire and/or are travelling a long distance.

Most airlines will carry bikes (if the plane is large enough) and they are often classed as "sports equipment" and are priced as, for instance, golf clubs or skis. Check with each individual airline regarding rules and costs etc. Generally, if the tyres are deflated slightly, the pedals removed and the handlebars moved through 90 degrees i.e. the bike is flat, that's all that's needed for the bike to be carried. It must be covered to prevent any oil and dirt coming into contact with the other hold luggage. Airlines differ, some are OK with a sheet of plastic and there are soft and hard bike cases on the market. A favourite trick of a friend of mine is to get a cardboard bike delivery box from a bike shop, wrap the bike and dispose of the cardboard at his destination. He then finds a bike shop at the other end to beg another box for the return trip.

If bags or boxes are used, it's necessary to agree where they can be left for the return leg. We bought second hand non rigid bike bags and agreed with the hotel in Berlin they would look after them until our return flight.

Remember to take all the necessary tools to reassemble the bike and a pump for the tyres!

***

We arrived, astonishingly, at the scheduled (and overly early) time at Bristol airport. Luckily our plane was delayed by over an hour, ensuring we had even greater contingency to allow for the non-existent difficulty of getting our bikes on the plane. We drank beer in the airport lounge and ate over-priced curry and chilli.

Once we had taken off, the flight was uneventful and we arrived at Berlin Schönefeld airport at about 22:30.

Berlin Schönefeld Airport (*Flughafen Berlin-Schönefeld*) is the secondary international airport in Berlin. It is the smaller of Berlin's two airports (Berlin Tegel Airport being the largest).

Schönefeld Airport was the major civil airport of East Germany (GDR) and the only airport in the former East Berlin. Part of Schönefeld's existing infrastructure is set to be incorporated into the neighbouring Berlin Brandenburg Airport, scheduled to open in late 2020. Schönefeld's then refurbished terminals are intended to be used until at least 2026 as part of the new airport.

A phone call to the nearby Hotel Albergo and Mario appeared to collect us in a small car as the minibus is being repaired. A couple of trips with Mario does the trick and just before 23:30 we are in the hotel bar drinking beer, served by Julia.

Distance cycled: 0km

Cumulative distance: 0km

Friday 2nd September - Berlin Schönefeld - Sachau

We were up for a rather pork-based breakfast at 08:00. After breakfast we collected our bikes (still in bags) from the cupboard under the stairs and went outside for a Bike re-mantling session which was a great success and we were ready to roll around 10:00.

The hotel were happy to hold onto our bags but there was limited space for 5 bike bags at the hotel and they asked that we pay €5 per bag per night to leave them there (this cost had never been mentioned before, but there is little space in the room and it seems bad manners to create a fuss). We managed to pack bags inside other bags so leave only two at a total cost of €40. We were advised that it would take only 20 minutes to cycle from Ostbahnhof to Haptbahnhof, so decided to train to the former rather than the latter and try to do this, enabling a view of some of Berlin's famous sights.

Unfortunately, confusion reigned at the Schönefeld railway station as we were unable to work out how to buy the requisite tickets (part of the confusion is how to add 5 people and 5 bikes). A man in a red hat finally took pity on us. He must surely have been a busy boy, given the number of bemused people milling around the machines and failing to work them out (a lad in front of us took an age because the machine disliked every single piece of Euro currency he tried). A lack of Teutonic thoroughness in this (though this is old East Germany).

We did manage to get all of us and our bikes onto the train, alighted at Ostbahnhof and cycled past the Berlin Wall and had a look at lots of Berlin Wall artworks; catching sight of the TV Tower.

The Berlin Wall was constructed in 1961 to separate West Berlin and East Berlin during the Cold War. All the differences between the countries made it a perfect place for people to express their opinions, especially their preferences and dislikes. In the 1980s, the wall was reconstructed and made 14 feet tall. Graffiting on the wall became popular for artists from all over the world and a place where tourists would go and admire the artwork. The West Berlin side of the wall had artwork completely covering the wall, while the East Berlin side was kept blank because people were not permitted to get close enough to the eastside of the wall to paint anything.

The Berlin Wall was one of the largest canvases in the world. Much of the artwork was not claimed by artists and remains anonymous. Because the wall was open to everyone, there were no restrictions on what artists could put on the wall. Over the past 30 years since the collection of artwork was started, much of the controversial artwork has been removed from the wall. Almost all of the wall has now been removed and it only exists in places such as

Potsdamer Platz, the East Side Gallery, and Bernauer Straße and many segments are now exhibited in other countries.

Our route took us via Alexanderplatz (with more than 360,000 visitors daily, Alexanderplatz is, according to one study, the most visited area of Berlin) and then via Unter den Linden to the Brandenberg Gate (where we saw Darth Vader).

Pedalling through the gate, we then cycled past the Reichstag; reconstructed by Norman Foster it is now the site of the German parliament.

We then cycled past some EU buildings, across the Spree to the Hauptbahnhof to catch our train to Lutherstadt Wittenberg. Against all the rules, we took our laden bikes down the escalators.

Our bikes were loaded onto the train but our tickets ha put as at the other end of the train and in first class. A friendly and attractive German lady was disconcerted by all 5 of us piling into the carriage (frankly, not looking like first class passengers), filling it to the brim. Actually it was **our** compartment but we let that rest. But she rose to the challenge and we chatted about this and that.

Although we were aware of the approximate time of the journey, we were surprised by the arrival of the train into Wittenberg and were told by our new German friend to be quick otherwise the train may leave with our bikes. We leapt nimbly from the train and hared its length, toting our panniers and ignoring the whistle signalling the train's departure. We managed to throw ourselves and bikes to the platform in time and were rewarded by a friendly wave from our new friend.

We dragged our bikes downstairs off the platform but found the way out was temporarily back upstairs. Eventually we were free and we started our serious cycling by stopping for lunch after less than a mile and drinking beer in Lutherstadt Wittenberg town square.

Lutherstadt Wittenberg, is on the River Elbe, 60 km north of Leipzig and 90 km south-west of Berlin.

Wittenberg is famous for its close connection with Martin Luther and the Protestant Reformation, for which it received the honorific *Lutherstadt*. Several of Wittenberg's buildings are associated with the events, including a preserved part of the Augustinian monastery in which Luther lived, first as a monk and later as owner with his wife Katharina von Bora and family.

It has a charming central square so we were happy to spend an hour or so recovering from the arduous journey!

We toured the few stalls that constituted a market on the opposite corner of the square and bought some nectarines for pudding.

Eventually we tore ourselves away and found the Elbe and its cycle path. It was not long before we reached a bridge over the river and were advised by a German cyclist to cross the bridge as that was the direction to Prague (our general target, in a 'we need to head east' kind of way). We followed these instructions, but, they didn't seem correct and a passing German hausfrau cyclist told us the first man was clearly an idiot and we should return over the bridge and turn right, in our original direction. Good start.

As predicted, it was very flat cycling. After a while, we stopped and drank coffee in Elster, while overlooking a ferry - the Fähre-Elster - that seemed to use a long piece of string and the river current to move between banks and connected the L127. A very cost effective method.

In fact it was a cable ferry, one of many we'd see along the way. This is a ferry that is guided (and in many cases propelled) across a river or large body of water by cables connected to both shores.

This was a reaction ferry, which uses the power of the river to tack across the current rather than a powered cable ferry, which uses an engine or electric motors.

A reaction ferry uses the reaction of the current of a river against a fixed tether to propel the vessel across the water. Such ferries operate faster and more effectively in rivers with strong currents.

Some reaction ferries operate using an overhead cable suspended from towers anchored on either bank of the river. Others use a floating cable attached to a single anchorage that may be on one bank or mid-channel. Where an overhead cable is used a "traveller" is usually installed on the cable and the ferry is attached to the traveller by a bridle cable. To operate the ferry either the bridle cable is adjusted or a rudder is used, causing the ferry to be angled into the current, and the force of the current moves the ferry across the river.

As the ferry cannot steer, a ramp is built at both ends and there is usually a set of controls facing in either direction.

Cable ferries are common where there is little other water-borne traffic that could get snagged in the cable or chains, where the water may be too shallow for other options, or where the river current is too strong to permit the safe crossing of a ferry not attached to the shore. Alignment of the platform at each end of the journey is automatic and, especially for vehicle ferries, safer than a free-moving ferry might be in bad conditions.

We also encountered reaction ferries on a later trip along the river Weser in 2018.

Elster is at the mouth of the Black Elster, where it empties into the Elbe. The area around Elster is very flat, indeed most of the land was flat, rising as we approached the Czech border. There are many flat areas; *Elbauen*, which at high water work as natural polders. During the so-called Flood of the Century in 2006, these natural polders were not high enough to keep the water back, leading to a great deal of the community being flooded. In 2004, a new landing stage was completed where Elbe cruise ships now stop.

Our target was the tiny burg of Sachau, near Priesitz and the Pension und Gasthof "Zur Müllerin" proprietor Frau Marcella Müller (their website claims it's "where the Elbe and Dubian heath marry").

This became signposted just before we crossed the river on another reaction ferry; the Elbe Fähre Pretzsch, a little further on. This connects the two halves of the L128. A German cyclist told us the Pension is a place of riotous music and dancing, but warned us that the owner would certainly try to fleece us over the number of drinks we consume. He kept us company for a while and then advised us of the right road to take. We passed an old and pretty little church on the way - Evangelische Kirche Priesitz and a wall strangely crennellated with squashes.

We found the Pension without trouble. Sachau having no obvious other attractions, we ate at the Pension. This involved Soljanka soup (very nice) and other stuff made by Frau Müller. Solyanka (Russian spelling) or "Settlers" Soup" is a thick, spicy and sour Russian soup that is common in Russia and other states of the former Soviet Union and certain parts of the former Eastern Bloc. It was one of the most popular dishes of the former East Germany.

We drank some beer while Herr Müller entertained us by playing clarinet karaoke; fortunately only 3 tunes (perhaps the only ones he knows). We drank some more beer. Then Herr Müller talked to us for some time, apparently Martin Luther once visited the church next door. Herr Müller also indicated the difficulty of being sure that UK bookings for 5 people for a week are genuine and encouraged us to try some short drinks. We plumped for one of two types and very nice it was too. Another inmate of the Pension spent the whole evening wearing a vest, only, on his upper body, though we found it a little chilly after a very hot day.

Distance cycled: 36km

Cumulative distance: 36km

Saturday 3rd September - Sachau - Belgern

Up for a rather pork-based breakfast at 08:00. Herr Müller sadly failed to overcharge us for drink and we were obliged to remark on the very good value and also paid in cash.

Another very hot day, that day's target was Belgern. We set off on a bit of a main road initially but we did get to see a windmill made of hay bales and a Trabby with flags left by the side of the road.

The Trabby or Trabant was produced from 1957 to 1990 by the former East German car manufacturer VEB Sachsenring Automobilwerke Zwickau. It is often seen as a symbol of the former East Germany and the collapse of the Eastern Bloc in general. The Trabant had a duroplast body mounted on a one-piece steel chassis (a so-called unibody), front-wheel drive, a transverse engine and independent suspension – unusual features in 1957 but it remained much the same until 1989 when it acquired a (licensed) Volkswagen engine; it was discontinued in 1991. The 1980s model had no tachometer, no indicators, no fuel gauge, no rear seat belts and drivers had to pour a mix of petrol and oil directly under the bonnet.

Called "a spark plug with a roof", over 3 million Trabants in a number of models were produced over nearly three decades with few significant changes in their basic design. Older models have been sought by collectors, the Trabant also gained a following among car tuning and rally racing enthusiasts.

The Trabant became "a symbol of the technological and social backwardness of the East German state" and a symbol of the GDR's serious flaws in the west after the fall of the Berlin Wall, when many were abandoned by their Eastern owners who migrated west. Unlike other cars manufactured in former eastern European countries i.e. the Lada Niva, Škoda Estelle, Polski Fiat (licensed from the Italian car manufacturer) and Yugo, the Trabant had negligible sales in Western Europe.

A Trabant could be bought for very little during the early 1990s, and many were given away. This particular one was just there, on an island in the middle of the road.

The ride was very pleasant with many apple trees and a few damson trees along the way as well as a *strange fruit* tree full of useful direction-signs to places such as the South Pole along the way.

As with most of the route along the river, it was very flat. Other interesting sights included a large Insect Hotel and later an orange rally-enabled Trabby complete with spoiler and purple tinted windows!

We reached Torgau for lunch, which, like most towns along our route, had a very large town square with a lovely renaissance town hall, historic town houses and a big fountain, all very pleasant. Torgau is best known as the place where, on 25th April 1945, U.S. and Soviet forces first met near the end of the Second World War.

We excelled ourselves by sitting outside an ice cream parlour for a coffee. Then we strolled across the square to the Goldener Anker Hotel beer garden and ordered beer. They immediately brought us a schnapps (or similar) and our beer - Schwarzbier - which was rather fine. *Schwarzbier*, or black beer, is a dark German lager-type beer with an opaque, black colour with hints of chocolate or coffee flavours and are generally around 5% ABV. These beers are similar to stout in that they are made from roasted malt, which gives them their dark colour. Needless to say as we are all beer fans and we were in Germany, we did sample many types of beer including Weißbier ("white beer", but the name probably derives from Weizenbier, "wheat beer"), which contains a significant proportion of malted wheat replacing malted barley.

We had lunch of various things including our new favourite Soljanka soup, followed by an excellent salad involving feta cheese. We drank another beer and then trudged around the town, considered an ice cream elsewhere, before deciding to go back to our regular place in the square and having some very nice yoghurt and fruit ice cream-y things.

In one of the shops we spotted a good map of the Elberadweg route so bought it (it might have been an idea to have one at the start, I suppose!) and an Army Shop (and tattoo parlour), which was fortunately closed, otherwise goodness knows what we might have been tempted to buy (an army?)! An odd looking 'cigarette machine' on the wall of a closed bike shop, turned out to be an inner tube dispenser – very thoughtful.

By the time we left we had been there for nearly four hours. Really hard these cycling holidays. Before leaving Torgau square, a short short-wearing elderly gent attracted our attention and asked us to guess his age. We politely suggested something in the 60s and eventually he announced he's 84-ish. We expressed amazement and he gleefully demonstrated his dancing ability by skipping, marionette-like, in front of us. We finally managed to tear ourselves away.

As mentioned earlier, Torgau is the place where, during the Second World War, United States Army forces coming from the west met forces of the Soviet Union coming from the east during the invasion of Germany on 25 April 1945. This is now remembered as "Elbe Day". Units of the American First Army and the Soviet First Ukrainian Front met on the bridge at

Torgau and at Lorenzkirch (near Strehla which was on the next day's agenda), 20 miles to the south. The unit commanders met the following day at Torgau for an official handshake. This marked the beginning of the line of contact between Soviet and American forces, but not the finalised occupation zones. In fact the area surrounding Torgau initially occupied by U.S. forces was later, in July 1945, given over to Soviet forces in compliance with the Yalta agreement. After the war, in 1949, a film entitled "Encounter at the Elbe" was released depicting this meeting of the two armies.

Torgau was one of the prisons where Reinhold Eggers spent his post war imprisonment after being sentenced by the Soviets. Eggers had been the security officer at Oflag IV-C during the war. Oflag IV-C is better known as Colditz Castle.

Two days after the official meeting it was re-enacted at Torgau for the press. As we left Torgau we passed a substantial stone monument and a small information board commemorating this event.

We continued on to Belgern, following good signs to Pension Sigwarth and passing amongst other things a stationary engine in a glass display case, in the front garden of a house. Generally there were many cyclists on the route, a few laden as we were but a lot of locals pottering around the area.

Pension Sigwarth was a little unprepossessing at first, but turned out to be a gem and is approved by the General German Bicycle Club (ADFC) so great for those on the Radweg.

We checked in and negotiated very steep steps up to the first floor where found our rooms with the bathroom boasting tasteful light grey grouting. A highlight of the Pension was the honesty fridge which was well stocked and cheap and which we investigated closely after showering.

We drank some beer from the honesty fridge and were joined by a Herr Klein and this afforded us some amusement given that we were the Huge party (the booking was made in the name of Hughes but there's an endearing German inability to understand that 'gh' is not pronounced) and Klein sounds like kleine, meaning small. So we were the Little and Large parties. Hilarious.

Herr Klein turned out to be a policeman from western Germany and is obviously well versed in interrogation techniques, learning everything about us and where we were going, while being very evasive about his own party's plans.

We were recommended a restaurant in town, which was OK and unsurprisingly served pork-based stuff. We sat outside and drank beer. Herr Klein joined us from his party and told us an old joke in English, which wasn't that funny even when told by a native English speaker so imagine its flatness when he told it.

Belgern was yet another lovely village, steeped in historical buildings and an obligatory fountain or two. The place was dominated by the church of St. Bartholomew (1512). A memorial stone in front of the church commemorated Martin Luther's visit in 1522

On our way back to the Pension we noticed much music going on up the road next to the fire station and were reminded that Herr Sigwarth was a part time fireman and this was its 40th anniversary. We investigated and found a tent full of pissed firemen and the remnants of a BBQ. We decided we would like to get a beer, but decided that they would not have welcomed us, as it was a private party. On returning to the Pension, we sat outside for a period, drinking beer and some local sweet wine from the honesty fridge.

Distance cycled: 47km

Cumulative distance: 83km

Sunday 4th September - Belgern - Meißen

Up for a rather pork-based breakfast at 08:00, another keenly priced night's accommodation (around €111 for the rooms plus €19 for the beer).

We took a look on our way out at the town square, which had in it a gigantic statue of a knight in armour. The was a 16m tall Belgian Roland, hewn out of stone in 1610. It is the only surviving Roland statue in the Free State of Saxony. The Roland is a statue of a knight with a bare sword and is considered a symbol of city rights. Roland statues are therefore - comparable to the court columns that are more common in southern Europe - in marketplaces or in front of town halls and can be found more often, especially in northern and eastern German cities. There are also other statues in Central Europe, Croatia and Latvia, as well as replicas in Brazil and the United States.

Heading out across the flood plain, we passed a house with sky blue roof tiles – weird.

We spotted a roadside sign offering coffees, so stopped in the charming garden/rubbish dump of a scruffy shed run by a scruffy couple. He was very friendly though and talked us through his array of homemade fruits-and fungi-of-the forest potions giving us free shots of home-made chilli vodka. It was frankly disgusting but had to be seen as a challenge...

This was another very hot day as we struck out for Meißen with again, a flat and wide vista on the route.

We passed through Strehla, another pretty town. Strehla is regarded as the point towards the end of World War II where at 11:30am on April 25, 1945, troops of the Western Allies heading east first encountered Soviet troops heading west. Lieutenant Albert Kotzebue of the 69th Infantry Division (United States) encountered a Russian on horseback at nearby Leckwitz, later identified as a trooper of a Soviet Guards rifle regiment. The later encounter on the same day at 4:40 p.m. in Torgau, would go into history books as the official link-up.

We stopped for lunch in Riesa (twinned with Rotherham) The town was rather undistinguished, although surprisingly it had small container port on the river and a window in the local 'hanging' style and decorated with pigs (or, you might say, decorated with pork).

In the centre of Riesa is a 25m tall, 234 tonne, cast-iron sculpture by Jörg Immendorff of an oak trunk, named *Elbquelle* (source of the Elbe). This was erected in 1999 and local folk call the sculpture by many other names, most notably "Rostige Eiche", which means "rusty oak".

Riesa is known locally for the *SACHSENarena*, a large hall which bizarrely hosted the European Sumo Wrestling Championship in October 2003 and the World Sumo Wrestling Championship in October 2004.

We managed to find a café/restaurant with bicycles on its roof so stopped there and had pork-based stuff. We drank some beer and watched someone come a cropper on their bike as they passed. He was using his mobile phone, so a very satisfying result. We spotted the Klein brigade as they biked past us, but they shiftily carried on, Klein himself feigning not to see us.

After the pork-based meal, we walked all of 20ft to an ice cream parlour, where we were served by a very pleasant and very brightly tattooed young lady, with some unsightly piercings around her nose. She also sported a bracelet made from part of a bicycle chain, to remind her of a bad accident she had had years previously. I'd have probably remembered anyway, if it had been me. There was a street phone box, or similar, with a large temperature display that was alternating with the local time. We noted that the temperature was climbing from 37 to 38, then 39. We took bets on it reaching 40, which it failed to do while we sat there, but, once we'd moved away about 20m, it suddenly made a dash for it, achieving it, but immediately feeling ashamed and retreating back to a chilly 39. Oddly, a companion box about 200m away showed the temperature as 33.

The route on to Meißen was fairly easy, punctuated by a stop to try to get some damsons from a tree, but most of the easy pickings had already been had. One of us accidentally left his sunglasses there and on returning found they'd already been taken by someone else. We also halted at a shack where we drank some beer.

We had observed many things that day, firstly that the locals keep bees in bulk, instead of hives they have a road trailer the size of a Luton van, filled with bees in plastic baskets. Presumably (and further research couldn't confirm this) the bees can be moved from area to area and crop to crop thereby pollinating a large area.

In a couple of places, including in one case the top of a tree, there were steel platforms for cranes or storks to build their nests on, something we'd never seen before, the assumption being to encourage nesting.

After a riverside beer in a very pleasant shed-based Biergarten, we crossed the river by ferry and the approach to Meißen was trouble free. We were beginning to enter a gorge now that would characterise the rest of the route and there were small vineyards on the steep sides. This area is known as Saxon Switzerland (German: *Sächsische*

Schweiz) and is a hilly climbing area and national park around the Elbe valley south-east of Dresden. Together with the Bohemian Switzerland in the Czech Republic it forms the Elbe Sandstone Mountains.

Saxon Switzerland alone has some 1,000 climbing peaks, as well as several hollows. The area is popular with local and international climbers.

In 1766, two Swiss artists, Adrian Zingg and Anton Graff, were appointed to the Dresden Academy of Art. From their new, adopted home they looked eastwards and saw, about a day's walk away, a hill range with a strange, flattish profile, without any actual summits. They felt the landscape was reminiscent of their homeland, the Swiss Jura, and reported in their exchange of letters on the difference between their homeland and "Saxon Switzerland".

Meißen looked as if someone had stuck a big white schloss (chateaux) on the side of the cathedral deliberately to obscure it. We stood under a bridge waiting for all of us to catch up and asked for directions to the right area for our hotel from a local who instructed us to cross the second "brucke", then the first, then the second. We thank him, waited until he was out of sight and crossed the bridge above us anyway.

Meißen was a larger place than we'd been used to over the last few days and is the home of Meissen porcelain and boasts the Albrechtsburg castle, the Gothic Meissen Cathedral and the Meissen Frauenkirche.

Meissen porcelain or Meissen china was the first European hard-paste porcelain. The production of porcelain in the royal factory at Meissen, started in 1710 and attracted artists and artisans to establish, arguably, the most famous porcelain manufacturer known throughout the world. Its signature logo, the crossed swords, was introduced in 1720 to protect its production; the mark of the swords is reportedly one of the oldest trademarks in existence. In English Dresden porcelain was once the usual term for these wares, especially the figures; this is because Meissen is geographically not far from Dresden and is the Saxon capital.

The Hotel Siebeneichen was found to be up the top of a very steep and very long hill and was a perfectly agreeable, though seemingly very quiet hotel. It also boasted tasteful light grey grouting in the bathroom. Thinking of the long drag into town, we decided to order a taxi and on arrival, chose a restaurant with outside tables overlooking the square.

We drank beer. Someone told us that the bells in the church tower in Meissen are made of porcelain, which surely means a fairly delicate strike is required.

We listened to them and perhaps they didn't sound too metallic. Further research upon returning home confirmed that the *Frauenkirche* (Church of Our Lady) bell tower, situated in the old market-place hosts the world's first porcelain carillon, manufactured in 1929 on the occasion of the town's 1000-years-jubilee.

Upon arrival of the bill, we put more than enough cash and (as we have discovered is usual here) the waiter moved to retain it all, keeping the excess as a tip. We had to insist that he gave us the change so we could determine the size of the tip. Which turned out to be pretty much all the change anyway.

We walked back to the hotel. It didn't seem too bad, to our mutual surprise, considering that we felt too knackered to walk down it.

Distance cycled: 60km

Cumulative distance: 143km

Monday 5th September - Meißen - Heidenau

Up for a rather pork-based breakfast at 08:00, unusually served in a bedroom with the bedroom furniture replaced by tables. Yet again a very reasonably priced night.

We had left the bathroom window open, but during a very heavy thunderstorm overnight this had swung wildly and swept various items to the floor, but then closed itself, so we were a bit nonplussed to find the bathroom swimming in water and nobody admitting to have had a midnight shower.

We biked down the hill into town, and headed for the Meissen factory, where we milled around the (mostly) ghastly chinaware. All requiring lots of effort to make and paint etc, but you'd need a schloss to put it in, as in a normal-sized house it would frighten the children, who would feel impelled to smash it.

There was a series of demonstrations showing the process of making the stuff, which was quite interesting, comprising three different rooms in which first we saw a bloke moulding a pot, secondly an attractive woman forming tiny flowers and adding things to larger pieces and finally someone painting a plate. My favourite bit was the English translation of biscuit (the soft mould-able form of the pottery before it's fired) to bisk-wit. The general view was that while skilled work, it must be really tedious and frankly not worth the candle, considering the hideous, overblown results.

On leaving it started raining and it continued to do so on and off all day, on our way to Dresden, then on to Heidenau, on the outskirts. One of us having failed to bring appropriate wet weather gear, had the previous day, found a large blue plastic bag, which he fashioned into a waterproof tabard. The first attempt at arm holes was an abject failure, making him look a little foolish, but a second attempt was more successful, and had the unexpected benefit that the original arm holes now provided ventilation.

There was a sizeable fleet of paddle steamers on this stretch of the river, and we had once hoped to get a ride on one of them just for the sake of it. This didn't work out, but they were nice to see, rather like big toys. They travelled quite quickly and it must be a giggle avoiding mud banks etc.

We passed through the small town of Coswig and entered Radebeul, a garden suburb of Dresden, sometimes called the "Nice of Saxony" for its pleasant landscape and mild climate.

The approach to Dresden was great; the town appeared in the distance and all the old buildings (many re-built after the war) remained visible all the way in. On the way we passed a sorry looking 'beach resort' complete with bussed-in sand, deckchairs and ice cream hut (=shed) - all completely drenched in the rain. We crossed an impressive wide road/tram bridge to the city walls and city gate, complete with buskers – a Teutonic brass ensemble. We saw a great fat bloke being pulled on a rickshaw by a thin bloke – which country are we in again?

Dresden was heavily bombed during World War II and the bombing by the RAF and the USAAF between 13 and 15 February 1945 remains controversial. On the night of 13–14 February 1945, 773 RAF Lancaster bombers dropped over 1,000 tons of incendiary bombs and nearly 1,500 tons of high explosive bombs on the city. The inner city of Dresden was largely destroyed. The high explosive bombs damaged buildings and exposed their wooden structures, while the incendiaries ignited them, denying their use by retreating German troops and refugees. Widely quoted Nazi propaganda reports claimed 200,000 deaths, but the German Dresden Historians' Commission, made up of 13 prominent German historians, in an official 2010 report published after five years of research concluded that casualties numbered between 18,000 and 25,000. The Allies described the operation as the legitimate bombing of a military and industrial target. Several researchers have argued that the February attacks were disproportionate. Mostly women and children died. When interviewed after the war in 1977, Sir Arthur Harris stood by his decision to carry out the raids, and reaffirmed that it reduced the German military's ability to wage war.

Meandering through this fairly small (rebuilt) old part of town we found ourselves in the Altmarkt square, which was full of a wooden market (i.e. sheds), like the German Xmas markets that have started appearing in the UK. We stopped at the first stall and ate a Rostbratwurst (Thüringen sausage) and drank some beer. Then we shared another Pfefferrostbratwurst (pepper bratwurst) which wasn't as good. We then tried eating quarkkrapfen (which is like an onion bhaji filled with custard) which didn't get a seal of approval. The friendly woman injecting the custard with a giant bench-mounted syringe, had a wry smile on her face, and no wonder. In fact quarkkrapfen are German doughnuts and they go by many names, Krapfen or Berliner.
Quarkkrapfen use Quark in the batter, Quark being made from butter milk but it is not a cheese and it is not a yogurt – technically. Most recognize it as a fresh cheese. However, it doesn't use any rennet or require any starter. Thus, not a cheese or a yogurt and it tasted like a cross between cream cheese and yogurt, a little sweet, a little tangy and very thick and smooth on the palate.

During this time, the rain stopped.

A miniature railway for small children was run by a – quite understandably – miserable-looking 'station master' in a peaked cap sitting in a tiny Perspex 'ticket office'.

We noticed there was a Dresden museum, and interestingly we felt the right way to do this, while on a cycling holiday, was to walk there with our panniers. Feebly, some of us protested that perhaps it would be easier to cycle, but off we trudged. We chortled about how amusing it would be if the museum was closed on a Monday. Which it was.

Back to the bikes, and off we headed to Heidenau, in the rain, which was now very steady. Part way, we came across what at first appeared to be a soggy dumped chaise longue, but was actually a purpose built fibreglass model so we reclined for a relaxed-looking photo in the rain.

On we went in the rain. At one point, in Laubegast, we stopped for a coffee, thinking the rain was set to get heavier. Instead it eased. After refreshing ourselves and re-starting, the rain became heavier again.

As we turned off the cycle path to head into Hedienau, the wind increased, the rain suddenly became torrential and we were soon very wet indeed. A friendly local at a bus stop directed us to the Hotel Reichskrone, which we were surprisingly heading directly for. During check in we dripped all over the forms we had to sign for the rooms. I was so wet that the receptionist, without a word, handed me a paper napkin to dry myself. Our rooms were, interestingly, 101, 202 and 303 and were very warm, which proved quite handy for drying all the sodden stuff. The bikes were locked in a wooden shack which was already very full of bikes, but we crammed ours in anyway. We decided to stay in the hotel rather than try to wetly find somewhere in the apparently (and as we discovered the following day, in reality) dull town. We met for a beer and stayed there to eat. Food was excellent, involving tender braising steak type meat, and cabbage and potatoes. We drank more beer. And wine. And shots, including Underberg, not very nice, and Jaegermeister, much pleasanter. We were the only people left downstairs after a while and the waiters seemed quite keen to get rid of us, but we stuck it out until quite late.

Distance cycled: 42km

Cumulative distance: 185km

Tuesday 6th September - Heidenau - Königstein - Czech Republic - Bristol

Up for a rather pork-based breakfast at 08:00. Most things were now dry, though my shoes remained moist for much of the day. I felt a little delicate after the drinks the previous night.

We found the bike shed was much less full and since they were in everyone else's way, our bikes had been carefully reorganised. Strangely, we did not see anyone else who looked remotely like a cyclist (not like what we did). I tried a test cycle before hitting the road and discovered that my front wheel quick release had been quick released, no doubt by people trying to get their bikes out past ours.

We headed east towards Bad Schandau, from where were to catch our train back to Berlin. The terrain was, as usual, very flat and well kept (though the route builders had a fondness for changing the surface every hundred yards, throwing in cobbles and uneven cement paving slabs wherever they fancied).

The scenery became less flat and much more interesting. Across the river on the top of the gorge side opposite, near Pirna, we spotted the 'must visit' bridge mentioned in some of the literature. It turned out it was several hundred feet above us between two pillars of natural rock, and looked like it may have been put there solely as a mirador.

It was the Bastei bridge named after a rock formation 194m above the Elbe River. Reaching a height of 305m above sea level, the jagged rocks of the Bastei were formed by water erosion over one million years ago. The Bastei has been a tourist attraction for over 200 years. In 1824, a wooden bridge was constructed to link several rocks for the visitors. This bridge was replaced in 1851 by the present *Bastei Bridge* made of sandstone. The rock formations and vistas have inspired several well-known artists.

Passing through Königstein with its imposing fortress/castle (during World War II the prisoner-of-war camp for Allied officers, Oflag IV-B, was located in the castle) we reached Bad Schandau in good time. As we had time to spare, we cycled on to the Czech border at Hřensko-Schmilka (Czech-German). We did this by crossing the river by ferry, and cycling down that side. When we reached the border, we crossed the river by another ferry, took photos at the border, then re-crossed and cycled back. Sensible people would have stayed on the one side.

At the station we asked several people where the carriage that would take our bikes was likely to be, so that we could stand at the correct spot on the platform. A consensus was reached, but then we asked someone else in the tourist information office which was handily located inside the station. She came out and pointed to a clear sign showing, for each train arrival time, the length of the train, and the position of the bike carriage, first class and the dining car. This was very useful and informative, and which of course we hadn't spotted. We stood at the exact spot for the bicycle carriage (E) and when the train arrived (on time, of course), we were somehow a carriage length away. However, it was no problem and we were quartered in the same carriage as our bikes, which meant they were very safe. So naturally, we left the compartment and went to have lunch in the dining car.

The train had started its journey in Hungary and we were served by a Hungarian waiter who recommended all things Hungarian: Hungarian Goulash Soup, Transylvanian goulash main course, and Hungarian chocolate tunnel (= supermarket style Swiss roll). It turned out to be much fun and tastier than perhaps one might have thought. He also brought some shots of something (probably Hungarian) and we certainly drank Czech and Hungarian beers.

We arrived at Berlin and had fun trying to work out where to get appropriate tickets for the short hop back to Schönefeld. It all worked out somehow and we were able to catch a slightly earlier train than expected, sharing the cycling carriage with lots of people all going to the airport.

At the airport, we walked to the Hotel Albergo to get the bags returned, which Mario did very swiftly, and he refused a tip. Typical of the kindness and generosity of everyone we'd met. We set to, dismantling the bikes, which went fairly smoothly and we were eventually allowed to pile them onto their own security conveyor belt. Oddly, the counter staff merely asked us how heavy they were and didn't weigh them. While waiting, a lad cycled into the check in area with 2 plastic bags hanging off his bike and a big rucksack on his back. He obviously intended to take all this stuff on a plane (ours as it happened) and we could see he was advised to take the pedals off and turn the handle bars, which he did on the floor in front of the check in desks. One of his plastic bags contained a large blanket, which he wrapped around the bike and sealed with some tape. It had been my notion to do similar, but the usefulness of a spare pannier in the bag outweighed the inconvenience of the bike bag.

We did the security stuff, where Mr Hughes is held up by the X ray machine recognising something electrical in his luggage. After about 4 scans, they narrowed it to his wallet and found a credit-card sized plastic magnifier which included a tiny battery which he'd forgotten he had, and which Bristol security either didn't find, or cared about. He left behind his phone and pen, but fortunately the security guy, who was now a close personal friend, hailed him and returned them

We found a shop/café/bar and drank some beer, we faffed with the spreadsheet and sorted out who owed whom, what. It all worked out rather easily.

Uneventful flight back, unloading all went well, and we collected my car and I dropped everyone around Bristol.

Distance cycled: 36km

Cumulative distance: 221km

Conclusions

This was considered to have been an excellent trip, it all went really well (it shows the benefit of detailed planning).

There were many upsides especially the friendliness of everyone we met. The accommodation was of the highest quality and cheap.

Despite being separated from our bikes by a train length on the train out of Berlin, all the trains were easy to use (once we had worked out how to buy tickets!).

The food was excellent and of course the beer was wonderful and varied.

We were on (and mostly stuck to) a designated bike path but everywhere was bike-aware and we had no bike breakages on route. It was surprisingly painless taking bikes on a plane.

Sadly there were a couple of downsides, a rather limited range of menu options and many pork-based breakfasts which did wear a little bit thin!

The cycling was flat and (until we hit the more hilly terrain) was a little dull (but very easy) in parts. The villages were, without exception, very pretty but some were rather dead with insufficient places to stop or buy odds and sods. While writing these notes, I looked for further information on places we visited but in many cases there was absolutely nothing to add!

Unfortunately, one of our bikes showed some damage on return with a slightly bent brake disc.

Although we only scratched the surface of this long distance route, cycling 221km of the total of 1,220km a feeble 18% of the route, hopefully it gives the reader a flavour of what could be achieved but we all had jobs (at the time) and families and couldn't really disappear for days on end. Maybe we will return in the future and complete another 18% but there's a lot more cycling out there to sample. We were happy pottering along, of course we could have completed 221km in a shorter time or travelled further but would we have had as much fun and been able to sample as much beer?

Cycling the Black Forest Cycle Way (Südschwarzwald-Radweg)

Adventures in three countries

"Every time I see an adult on a bicycle I no longer despair for the future of the human race" - H.G. Wells

Introduction

After some pub discussions, we agreed we would again travel to a country other than France, a country that embraces cyclists and cycling and is full of wonderful cycling routes and of course plenty of cheese and wine. Germany was chosen as it also has many cycling routes, plenty of wine and beer although it is not so great on the cheese front! After some research, we found Germany has many excellent routes, mainly along rivers i.e. Elbe, Rhine and Weser but we were intrigued by the circular route round the Black Forest with the potential to move between three countries, that was it - decision made.

What were we about to attempt?

The South Black Forest Cycle Path (Südschwarzwald-Radweg) is a 264km bike path around the Southern Black Forest in the Baden-Württemberg region of Germany. There are a number of optional side trips to the Petite Camargue in Alsace and north-western Switzerland near Basel but we decided to cycle through Basel then deviate north west into eastern France to make a longer and more varied route.

The route is mainly on asphalted or otherwise well-developed agricultural and forestry paths and can be easily completed in three to four days. As we had longer, we added a diversion into France.

The highest point is 885m above sea level and is considered the starting point. Luckily for us, there is a train that takes cycles 17km uphill to near the highest point from Kirchzarten to Hinterzarten. After this point the circular route does not have any significant uphill sections but many downhill and many flat sections i.e. "downhill" all the way to Basel. As it's a circular route, it can be started and stopped anywhere.

***

The full route, assuming a start in Hinterzarten in the Upper Black Forest running clockwise, follows the following route: Wutach valley via Titisee-Neustadt,

Lenzkirch, Bonndorf, Wutach, Stühlingen, Eggingen and Wutöschingen. Here the path takes you into the valley of the Upper Rhine and continues via Lauchringen, Waldshut-Tiengen, Laufenburg (Baden), Murg, Bad Säckingen, Schwörstadt to Rheinfelden (Baden). From there, there's a slightly hillier option via Dinkelberg to Lörrach, Schallbach and Kandern and Schliengen to Bad Bellingen. There's a flatter option (which we took) continuing along the High Rhine over the old Rhine bridge to Switzerland to Rheinfelden AG, Kaiseraugst, Pratteln, Muttenz and Birsfelden to Basel.

From Basel we struck out into France (more of that later) but the official route turns into the French Huningue (Petite Camargue) and over the Dreiländerbrücke back to the German Markgräflerland, starting from Weil am Rhein then visiting Bad Bellingen, Neuenburg am Rhein, Müllheim, Heitersheim, Ehrenkirchen, Pfaffenweiler and Eringen, returning to Freiburg im Breisgau.

In 2013/14, the Southern Black Forest Cycle Path was awarded 4 stars by the ADFC (General German Bicycle Club). This classification was confirmed in 2017 and the 45km variation bypassing Basel via Rheinfelden via Lörrach and the Dinkelberg has now also been classified by the ADFC.

The route is way marked and well signposted with the logo of Südschwarzwald-Radweg. This is a cyclist whizzing downhill with "Südschwarzwald-Radweg" written across it. The route also shares space with a few other national, local and EuroVelo routes i.e. 6 which also have their own signs and logos. Other routes come and go and there were a few rather cluttered signposts showing other route logos but if you concentrate on one it's easy to follow. Additionally, there are plenty of general cycle signs between places with distances marked in km.

***

There are many places to stay along the route but our preferred place to stay is in a tent. Campsites in Germany, especially in the touristy areas, are plentiful. As it was August, we assumed it would be hot and sunny so carrying a lightweight tent each we were good to go. We didn't book sites in advance of the trip but did have a couple of camp site guides with us so we knew where there would be one (or so we thought!).

The route was manageable on a road or a hybrid bike; no need for a mountain bike with big knobbly tyres. Arriving in the area is fairly easy, with good rail services to the major cities i.e. Freiburg and Basel and decent road links.

Navigation is easy as already mentioned but additionally we had a selection of maps (mainly for the French section) and the Bikeline Guide

"Südschwarzwald-Radweg", which although in German, was invaluable as it contains excellent maps with campsites clearly marked.

We debated about how to transport ourselves and our bikes to the Südschwarzwald-Radweg. We had hired on a previous trip to the Canal du Midi but the bikes were not great and we had flown with bikes on a trip to the river Elbe via Berlin but there's the issue of what to do with the bag or other covering on arrival. Trains were an option but it's a long way from Bristol and we didn't have the time for a very long train journey. So after finding a potentially good bike hire place offering cycles geared up for the route, indeed they advertised it as an option, we went along the hiring route. Additionally, the plane from Bristol was too small to take bikes.

So that's it, on with the adventure!

Fri 30th August - Bristol to Freiburg

There were only four of us at this stage, one was to join us later intending to meet us in Switzerland.

We had to be up at stupid-o-clock for the 06:40 BMI flight from Bristol to Frankfurt, everything was on time but the go to gate/stay in lounge/get up/sit down announcements were very confusing.

There were only 19 passengers on the 60-seat Embraer, plus our hostess Courtney, who admitted this was a typical load and probably not enough to sustain the service. She was hoping things would pick up after the holiday season when the business traffic would increase. Unfortunately, she was correct as trying to get home from a trip to Hamburg in 2018 we were delayed for a day as BMI unfortunately went bust due to lack of passenger numbers and our flight was cancelled.

Frankfurt airport is like any other big and busy airport, as we had an hour or so to wait for our train to Freiburg, we stopped for breakfast.

The train to Frieburg was punctual and very full so we had to stand until the change at Mannheim. The onward connection was conveniently on the same platform and there was plenty of room on the next train.

Arriving in Freiburg we decided to grab some lunch before going to collect the bikes. Luckily the railway station is very central so we didn't have very far to stagger with our cumbersome bags. We dropped into pretty much the first place we found - an Italian; Ristorante Pizzeria Antica. We had already accustomed ourselves to thinking in German, so the barrage of Italian interspersed with German and French caused meltdown; we replied in Spanish. The waitress said 'cheers' in all the languages of Europe.

***

At the bike hire - Radstation Freiburg - right in the centre of Freiberg next to the railway station we met Fernando, who really is Spanish and who told us he had both Icelandic and American children and that his wife was a 'souvenir of Berlin'. He also recounted what he believed to be a joke about his mother and chicken soup! We laughed politely and remained mystified. He told us the bikes were 'very worried' because we were so late.

Never mind worried, the bikes were certainly weird. On the one hand they were sound, almost new, spotlessly clean, identical Giant tourers, European upright style, with proper pannier racks yet they had three braking systems - surely one too many - the third being to pedal backwards to engage the third brake. The lights were a bit intermittent, hub-dynamo driven but we assumed we wouldn't be needing those and the gears were excellent seven-speed Sturmey-Archer style internal hub gears. As in all European bikes the brakes are reversed with the front being on the left but after a couple of km we were very used to them.

We had two large bags in the hold of the plane, each holding a couple of panniers and tents with our second pannier as cabin luggage meaning fewer checked in bags making it cheaper. We had already agreed with Radstation Freiburg that they would kindly look after the two large bags while we were away.

We loaded up and set off over the 'Bike Bridge' to ride all of 1km to the campsite - Camping Hirzberg. After 100m we stopped to review the lack of quick-releases on the wheels. You would need a decent spanner to get them off so we sent a text to the Bristol-based tourer to get him to bring one! The Radstation Freiburg provided pump, spare tubes and some basic tools so we would be fine.

The campsite was on a surprisingly steep hillside with many trees and was therefore extensively terraced. The tent-camping areas seemed a bit of an afterthought compared to the campervan areas and our pitch although carpeted with woodchips was quite conveniently placed.

After showers we toddled into the old town (Altstadt), an attractive place and reasonably lively looking. Busy and largely car-free, Altstadt is

Freiburg's historic heart, known for its cobblestone streets, tiny streams and preserved medieval gates. Bertold's Fountain, a post-war equestrian statue, is a popular meeting spot. Landmarks include the huge Gothic Freiburg Münster cathedral and Adelhauser Neukloster, a cluster of centuries-old convents. Upscale German restaurants, laid-back taverns and beer bars are dotted around the area.

We were taken by the tiny streams or "Freiburg Bächle" crisscrossing the streets. The Freiburg Bächle are small water-filled runnels, supplied with water by the river Dreisam. They can be seen along most streets and alleyways in the old city, being one of the city's most famous landmarks. The word *Bächle* comes from the German *Bach*, meaning stream.

First documented in the 13th century, the Bächle once served as a water supply and were used to help fight fires. In the 19th century they were seen as obsolete and most of them were covered with iron plates. The Bächle were seen by many (among them the ADAC) as a traffic hazard due to their original location in the middle of the road and as a consequence they were moved to the edge of the roads in 1852.

It is local superstition that if you accidentally step in the Bächle, you will marry a Freiburger. We managed to avoid steeping in any!

In 1973 the city centre of Freiburg was made a pedestrian zone with tram traffic which meant the Bächle did not pose a significant traffic inconvenience anymore even though some of them actually run parallel to the tram tracks.

Freiberg is a university and mining town and is a so-called *Große Kreisstadt* (large county town). Its historic town centre has been placed under heritage conservation and is a chosen site for the proposed UNESCO World Heritage Site known as the Ore Mountain Mining Region. For 800 years, the town was dominated by the mining and smelting industries but in recent decades it has restructured into a high technology site in the fields of semiconductor manufacture and solar technology.

We slowly discovered that it was not so easy to get a table for four, partly because of Chelsea v. Bayern Munich on the telly (UEFA Super Cup, 2-2 at FT and 5-4 to Bayern on penalties - not that we stayed to watch). We found one place eventually and there was not much choice food-wise either, burgers or Flammeküche (thin pizza). It was all ok and we managed to eat a couple of Flammeküche after which we walked back and fell asleep and slept well after our very early start that morning.

Distance cycled: 1km

Cumulative distance: 1km

Saturday 31st August - Freiburg to Ewattingen

We rose early and ate from the 'breakfast buffet' which was a small shelf of individually-priced bread, butter, jam, Philadelphia, juice etc. within the very small camp shop. The harried reception staff also made the hot drinks, added the cost up on calculators, took the money and did the clearing up slowly but there was relaxed eating at outside tables.

We headed out past the Youth Hostel to join the Südschwarzwald-Radweg proper, then alongside the river Dreisam, following the little cyclist sign that would become very familiar.

After 9km we reached Kirchzarten, where we bought bottle cages (having not realised there wouldn't be any on the bikes) in what turned out to be the best bike shop of the trip.

We had decided to take the train from Kirchzarten to Hinterzarten, although it was a short trip of about 17km, it lifted us up about 1km in height to the highest point on the route. Many cyclists choose to do this rather than slog up the hill and it meant the route to Basel on the Rhine was largely downhill or flat making for some wonderful cycling.

We easily found the station and the ten minute wait was used up struggling to buy tickets one at a time from a pedantic ticket machine. While waiting, we chatted to an Estonian who had just cycled all the way up through Italy - no doubt he recognised kindred spirits.

The train was very crowded (with bikes mainly) as it generously lifted us up the hill and deposited us in Hinterzarten. We celebrated by stopping immediately for coffees - and Black Forest Gateau. The latter, Herr Kipling style, was about 70% whipped cream by volume and was brown-coloured rather than chocolate-flavoured although the steeped cherries were quite nice. We did not know it at the time, but this would be our first and last Black Forest Gateau of the trip.

Prior to the trip, we assumed (wrongly) that Black Forest Gateau was named after the Black Forest and we would be gorging ourselves on it for a week. According to one school of thought, the name is derived from the speciality liquor of that region, known as *Schwarzwälder Kirsch(wasser)* which is distilled from tart cherries. This is the ingredient, with its distinctive cherry pit flavour and alcoholic content, that gives the dessert its flavour.

Cherries, cream and Kirschwasser were first combined in the form of a dessert in which cooked cherries were served with cream and Kirschwasser, while a cake combining cherries, biscuits and cream (but without Kirschwasser) probably originated in Germany. We now assume that what was on offer was purely for tourists and why it wasn't up to our exacting standards! Typically, Black Forest gateau consists of several layers of chocolate sponge cake sandwiched with whipped cream and cherries and decorated with additional whipped cream.

Had we had more time and as people who like a good museum we might have visited one of the two museum attractions in Hinterzarten, namely The Black Forest Ski Museum (opened in 1997) covers the beginning of skiing and the early techniques and equipment used on the nearby Feldberg or the museum of ancient agricultural engineering (2004). But we didn't.

***

Despite the good efforts of the train there was a bit more uphill to go before we crossed farmland - scattered with many noisy cows wearing bells. Then we descended a gentle, pretty woodland route down into Titisee, a little resort by the eponymous lake.

The Titisee lake covers an area of 1.3 sq km and owes its formation to the Feldberg glacier, the moraines of which were formed in the Pleistocene period and nowadays form the shores of the lake. The lake's outflow, at 840m above sea level, is the River Gutach, which merges with the Haslach stream to form the Wutach flowing eventually into the Upper Rhine.

Looking cheerful but strangely subdued, this was a place more suited to the middle-aged than to we youngsters - so we moved swiftly on. We then followed 18km of well-designed, not too hilly cycling through fairly dramatic countryside with forested hillsides and deep valleys occasionally following the river Gutach. We saw many cyclists, mostly middle-aged couples on e-bikes. At Neustadt we caught a glimpse of a steam-hauled train going in the opposite direction.

Finally the route ran into Lenzkirch (a lovely town with a huge town hall!), whence it would double back on the opposite side of the valley - but not before we stopped for lunch in the 'pub garden' of a guest house. The waitress' advice was Teutonically confident - *yes* we could cut across that way to join the outbound path and *yes* the campsite at Ewattingen was *definitely* still open *for certain*. That sounded good and we relaxed our plans a bit.

As we left town the road was rather trafficy but a couple of km later we were able to drop down onto a disused railway that was the official route, joining it at a viaduct, or was it a bridge? It was the Klausenbach Viadukt in fact, built in 1906; the main span is of the 'fish-belly' beam design and as such, very unusual and is 47m long and 22m high. The *Bähnle* cycle path leads across it and we joined that as part of our route.

We pressed on, bypassing Gündelwangen and skirting Bonndorf to where we detoured left across farmland, pretty with the occasional woodland and arrived in Ewattingen in two parties. One party went left towards the camping, dropping steeply into the west end of the village where three farmer types sat on a bench. 'Is there camping here?' was met with 'there used to be' and advice on how to get to Stühlingen where the next nearest site should be.

The eastern party went to the Gasthaus and found out the same, also that the Gasthaus was full. As we contemplated a further 17km ride, a waitress in a flouncy Bierkeller-style dress walked out to her VW Golf and told us there was another hotel around the corner. Which, it turned out, had loads of space and a garage opposite to put the bikes in! We could have a room each in fact, mostly en suite and for €32/head including breakfast.

We had a celebratory beer, put the bikes away and registered just as the light faded and the drizzle started. We met some more of the friendly family at the garage, where they were varnishing all the boards from the balcony - bet they wish they hadn't started! We felt very pleased with our decision even though the rooms smelled strongly of the cowshed over the road, but hey. Showers, some beer, more beer, dinner, wine, bed.

Distance cycled: 56km

Cumulative distance: 57km

Sunday 1st September - Ewattingen to Rheincamping Waldshut

We woke up duly refreshed in our luxury accommodation. The rain had passed but not so the smell of cows! We enjoyed a good continental breakfast, packed and headed off, sticking to the scenic detour rather than retracing our steps. Ewattingen was another beautiful village full of lovely farmhouses characteristic to the area and was dominated by a magnificent 16th century castle.

6km later at Blumegg there was a glimpse between houses of a gorge and a small boy on a bike bade us good morning. Thereafter there was a highly enjoyable 3km steep and bendy downhill to a bigger road, passing an interesting-looking three-wheel watermill/museum on the way into Grimmelshofen. Then we made some easy distance off-road beside the river all the way into Stühlingen - a place almost completely shut. This extra leg wouldn't have been too bad last night but we were glad we didn't bother.

Behind us the sky was black and shortly after we arrived at the one open café-bar the rain started, becoming a very heavy downpour. We were forced to retreat under a big umbrella as the staff hurriedly moved the cushions indoors. We had another coffee and when the rain thinned so we moved on, some in raingear, some not. At a pause for an ATM an elderly man asked us about the trip and then for some reason wanted to demonstrate he could count to ten in all the languages of Europe. Thankfully we were ready to move on after Turkish...

The route continued alongside the river Wutach and was easy going if uneventful with much of it traffic-free. We passed through Eberfingen and by Eggingen, through Wutöschingen where the river became more of a canal. The lower Wutach valley was straight, wide-bottomed and very densely populated. The river forms the border between Germany and Switzerland for two sections that total about 6km, after which it is canalised.

Continuing on between Horheim and Schwerzen, we had Lauchringen in our sights for lunch, but apart from an expensive hotel it looked rather closed so we pressed on to the larger Tiengen on the banks of the river Rhine and the inward route deposited us at a sizeable café/bar/ice cream parlour. Although even this was only just opening, it seemed.

It was getting hot and sunny again at this point and as we consumed our conservative beers, we sniggered at the fools ordering huge ice cream sundaes around us. Lunch was drawn out with pizzas and beer and lots of wasps! A woman at the next table was trying to kill them by clapping them between her hands. She usually missed, so the area was full of annoyed wasps (she complained it was because the wasps were too slow but we thought she must have meant too quick?)! Before she left, she invited us to Switzerland next year for the festival in Bad Zurzach. Following some post holiday research, it seems that apart from a kid's festival and a Röschti (Rosti) festival there didn't seem anything we'd like to attend.

    Finally, we succumbed to temptation and ordered huge ice cream sundaes.

    Eventually we set off on the final 6km leg to the campsite (Rheincamping-Waldshut), with the Wutach joining the Rhine halfway through this leg. The campsite was well ordered and seemed to be mostly composed of caravans converted into shacks by the addition of awnings, Jerry-built extensions, carports, fences, toilet-sheds and so on. In fact it took a while to spot the caravans underneath it all! One of these shack-structions even had a pretty village pump, marred only by a big 'not drinking water' placard. In the centre of the square of these little empires, village-green style, was the 'tent area' - totally unstructured which made it difficult to decide where to pitch. We paid and camped but unfortunately there was no mention of breakfast.

    Most of the other campers were also cyclists. Rheincamping-Waldshut is actually 2.5km before the small town of Waldshut itself and there was not much of a settlement nearby so we decided to eat in the campsite restaurant. It was standard fare, apart from extensive use of the Pfifferling (yellow chanterelle) sauce and we discussed the risks of commercial mushroom-growing. We carried on with a few drinks after the meal but when no one else was left the staff got themselves some drinks and we were asked to leave. There being nothing else to do now, we got an early night.

Distance cycled: 46km

Cumulative distance: 103km

Monday 2nd September - Rheincamping
Waldshut to Basel

We were up very early and found the restaurant was shut and reading the notice we found it was very, very shut, on Mondays. Presuming it would be open later with some breakfast for the campers, we decided to walk along the Rhine towards Waldshut, to see if a cup of tea was to be had (it wasn't).

The restaurant finally opened but despite the staff having nothing else to do, if you hadn't ordered breakfast the night before you could not have any, not even a cup of tea.

As there was no point hanging around, we struck camp and headed for Waldshut. We were all looking forward to meeting our absent friend at some yet-to-be-agreed point and had been exchanging texts with him earlier as he was boarding in Bristol. The Germany party's money was on him not being bothered to leave Basel, given he had been up so early.

The route was a pleasant ride along the river bank and as soon as we were in Waldshut we happened across a baker's shop with a very cheery woman baker. Coffees, pastries and much cheeriness later, we negotiated lots of road-works and as we passed out of town the path rose well up above the Rhine and provided great views of both.

The route continued along the German bank of the Rhine passing through Dogern and at Albbruck we stopped for coffee in the square of the large church - Church of Saint Joseph. Then we cycled on through Laufenburg, Murg and Bad Säckingen, where I managed to cycle into a big pile of cardboard boxes, to local consternation.

When we reached the Rhine, there was an impressive covered wooden bridge which we cycled across for the sake of it and saw the unoccupied Swiss customs office in Stein. We returned to Germany and continued.

The bridge in question; Holzbrücke Bad Säckingen (German) or Säckingerbrücke (Swiss); connects the German city of Bad Säckingen with the village Stein in Switzerland. The covered bridge spans about 200m over the Hochrhein and is the longest roofed wooden bridge in Europe and is listed as a national registered monument in Switzerland (Kulturgut von nationaler Bedeutung im Kanton Aargau).

The bridge was built in 1272 and was destroyed several times (1570, 1633, 1678). The current bridge was completed in 1700. Originally a road bridge, the bridge is now only open for pedestrians (and cyclists!) since a nearby bridge the Fridolinsbrücke (Swiss name: Rheinbrücke Stein) was opened in 1979 for road traffic.

Near Schwörstadt we saw a great sownder of swans and noticed a couple of local people seemed to be calling some individuals by name. Then we came to a level crossing and a slightly difficult road crossing - about the only one in the whole week and finally we arrived into Rheinfelden (fields of the Rhine), high above the Rhine and is home to Feldschlösschen, the most popular beer in Switzerland. Following more texts, this was where we arranged to meet our friend, who was coming out by train from Basel, via Frieburg to hire a bike and all his luggage. It was also where the route crosses into Switzerland.

We assumed as there is only one bridge in town, it was a good place to meet having assumed he would be coming out from Basel on the Swiss side. Sadly, when he got out of the train - on the German side - he was instead given directions to the motorway bridge 3km downstream. Although he soon spotted the problem, this all caused a bit of a delay, but we met eventually. We had lunch near the bridge on the Swiss side, a very nice lunch accompanied by some Feldschlösschen. Having no Swiss Francs, as we were 50m from the border, the café accepted Euros at a decent rate. Indeed, we managed to stay overnight in Basel with no need for Swiss Francs by using credit cards.

We pressed on after lunch, conscious that this was to be the longest day, in kilometres at least. The route out of Rheinfelden was not particularly clear and was mostly alongside a busy road. We moved gradually away from the Rhine, passing Kaiseraugst and Augst and through Pratteln and Muttenz. The route was not very nice (we were later told it would have been more pleasant to stay on the German side). It was very piecemeal, not exactly hard to follow but slow going as the cycleway worked its way round, under or over endless industrial plants and big roads including the Swiss/German border. Here traffic was being held up at customs. It struck us as slightly odd as Switzerland not being an EU member we could cycle across the border seemingly willy nilly carrying large panniers each with no border checks yet road traffic was subject to possible checks. Like many EU countries, Switzerland is part of the Schengen area where more relaxed border controls exist.

There were some interesting sights amongst the industry on the way such as a garden given over to a large-gauge model railway, fields of sunflowers and the outskirts of the Basel tram system.

After cycling through a large area of sports facilities we arrived into the traffic of Basel. Eventually we were in the centre of town and after an accidental foray up a flyover and back, we were again on the banks of the Rhine. We were following signs for the Basel Paper Mill, which was near the youth hostel. The paper mill is a papermaking, museum including the art of book printing and writing in general. The museum is located in a carefully restored building that began its life as a paper mill 500 years ago.

The Rhine was very impressive at this point, wide and quite fast when viewed from the roadway that runs well above it along the bank. We were surprised to see a number of people being washed down the river, some with floats to hang on to, others without. Every now and again these heads were bobbing directly towards a sizeable cargo barge or ferry, steaming up against the river current. The vessels seemed to have to slow right down and avoid the humans, who had of course little or no control in the matter.

This is Rhine swimming and is apparently a refreshing treat on a hot summer day. Strong swimmers can get in between the Wettsteinbrücke and Johanniterbrücke bridges and let the current take them downriver carrying a colourful Wickelfisch – a swim bag in the shape of a fish; invented in Basel – to keep clothes dry. We would try something similar but more low key the next day.

Basel is a lovely city, well worth a visit and it's where the Swiss, French and German borders meet.

It also has suburbs in France and Germany. The official language of Basel is (the Swiss variety of Standard) German, but the main spoken language is the local Basel German dialect.

The city is known for its many internationally renowned museums, ranging from the Kunstmuseum, the first collection of art accessible to the public in Europe (1661) and the largest museum of art in the whole of Switzerland; Fondation Beyeler.

Basel is Switzerland's second-largest economic centre after Zürich and in 2019 Basel was ranked among the ten most liveable cities in the world by Mercer together with Zürich and Geneva.

We checked into the Youth Hostel (booked from the UK) which proved to be both an excellent building and a bustling place, mainly with schoolchildren including several in wheelchairs, with their helpers. The Youth Hostel had a moat, a dedicated bike store in the basement and a sizeable collection of Swiss knives for sale; ideal for children! We had booked a bunk room and it was all to a pretty high standard, clean and smart.

An acquaintance, a keen cyclist who lives in Basel and is now retired, was joining us for the evening and for the next morning's cycling, as 'local guide'. He arrived (by bike) as planned and after we had showered, led us on foot along the river and over a bridge (both banks are in Switzerland at this point) to a fun restaurant - Restaurant Zur Linde - where beer was dispensed by the customer from a tap on the table itself. When dispensed by fools, it comes out 90% foam to 10% liquid. So despite a seemingly unlimited supply of beer we only managed a litre each in the whole evening! The food was excellent, with goulash one of the options. After a fine evening, we were guided back through some of the old city. Basel was definitely nicer than its 'industrial' reputation suggests.

Distance cycled: 70km

Cumulative distance: 173km

Tuesday 3rd September - Basel to Ruffach

Following a very good night's sleep and not having heard a peep from the multitude of kids, we headed for the restaurant which was not quiet at all. It was self service and there was a wide variety of stuff available, with a strong emphasis on the Swiss dairy industry.

When we had packed and retrieved the bikes from underground, our friend arrived on cue and we departed, continuing along the Rhine, through some picturesque old town and out through interesting (and neat, clean) industrial areas, to look at a couple of landmarks.

The Dreiländereck (three countries corner) is a pointy monument to the triple point of the borders and lies right on the Rhine. The tripoint itself is located in the middle of the river Rhine. The monument dedicated to it is in Swiss territory, on a point of land approximately 150m to the south-east. It can be conveniently viewed from the Tri-national Footbridge (which links Weil am Rhein, Germany and Huningue, France). We played about on the bridge for a while but actually needed to retrace our steps and continued in Germany and carried on through industrial areas to the Yacht Club café.

After a break we set off for the river-swimming area near Istein, about 15km north (downstream on the Rhine) from the Youth Hostel. We were told we should try to swim to the other side of the river where the current is fast and would carry the swimmer down over rapids before slowing and allowing the swimmer to come back ashore 1-200m away. Well that was the theory. Some of us didn't like the look of it. In fact there was no hope of getting to the other side as the river was much too fast, so those who braved the waters were swept, to a greater or lesser extent, down waterfalls! We survived, with bruises.

We were clambering across a rocky barrier, installed when the Rhine was canalised (running parallel) to allow large vessels to sail to Basel. Dams were installed between 1817 and 1870 and the Rhine was canalised between 1925 and 1980 (The Grand Canal of Alsace) leaving the "Old Rhine" for us to play in.

Fortunately, there was also a wimps option of getting into the water below the waterfalls and rapids and being washed down for a time to the gentle bit. This was very pleasant in itself but disgorged the swimmer at the fat old persons nudist beach which was not a sight for the faint-hearted.

At this point, we deviated from the official Sudschwarzwald-Radweg and headed into France. We debated whether to cycle all the way to our destination for the evening; Rouffach ('Roof-rack') or use a train for part of it which would have entailed retracing our steps to some extent. It was not unanimous but we agreed to cycle on. However, we also decided to stay at Rouffach for two nights, meaning we could do some of the wine route the next day without all our luggage.

The river-bank path was closed northward for works of some sort and we didn't know for how far, so we had to head east into Germany to bypass the problem. We took a route passing through Istein; Kleinkems; Rheinweiler; Bamlach and to Bad-Bellingen which was no doubt much further off-route than was actually necessary but we didn't have good signage as we were off-route. Catch 22.

In Bamlach (a lovely, very German village), we called at the butchers shop and yes, the butcher's wife would make us baguettes to order, of cheese and/or meat and/or cucumber. We ate these outside by the shop's sign - a life-size 'bronze' of a sow.

In Bad-Bellingen there was no signage for the cycle-route at all, we had a pointless conversation with some people who didn't live there and then decided to take a slalom to get down to river level. Well most of us did, one who shall remain nameless, still out to impress, cut a corner too sharply and catapulted off into the undergrowth!

Back on the Rhine path we soon reached our crossing point at Neuenburg am Rhein. We were in France! We then crossed the Rhine flood plain, it was a bit of a slog but flat and with straight roads. We headed north through Bantzenheim and Munchhouse where we stopped at the baker (Artisan Boulanger) for drinks and cakes, taken outside next to the church (Église Sainte-Agathe Munchhouse). Then we journeyed on through Hirtzfelden, turning west through Niederentzen to Rouffach. It was hot, very flat being a flood plain and not hugely exciting cycling.

Rouffach (German and Alsatian: *Rufach*) lies along the Alsatian wine route (*Route des Vins d'Alsace*). Its vineyards produce one of the finest Alsatian wines: the *Grand Cru* Vorbourg.

Rouffach turned out to be quite a pretty town with many ancient buildings, including a church (*Notre-Dame de l'Assomption*)with two towers and a fancy bell-tower. One of the paired towers was clearly incomplete. We speculated war damage but it turned out they just never finished it, stopping once the clock was in. There was also a Witches' Tower, a relic of the Inquisition and which was used as a prison. Madame at the campsite (Camping Municipal Alsacia) was very welcoming and provided a town map and info about the restaurants and cafés. We booked in for two nights and bought jetons for the hot showers. We did not however read the rules about 'total silence after 10pm'.

We had beer as we put the tents up but the ground was like rock so we used stones as 'hammers' and all was well.

After showers we headed into town where in fact, most places were already closed. When we asked at Les Trois Colonnades the waitress had to go and ask the chef if it was ok to let us in! Fortunately we were admitted, had an aperitíf of crémant d'Alsace, then excellent food including trout, accompanied by local pinot gris (white) and pinot noir (red) wines. Chef, who by now we knew was the waitress' husband, came out to apologise for running out of a particular strawberry pudding. We all had a jolly good chat and ordered a similar alternative plus a bottle of pudding wine and some digestífs, including one flavoured with églantine. We couldn't work out what this was but it led to a great conversation with our hosts (it's rose hips from wild roses, we now know). The best thing was the whole conversation was conducted in French and we were all pals, entente cordiale at its best. When we left, we were surprised to be given a bottle of the crémant as a gift.

When we arrived back in camp, we obviously had to drink the crémant while it was still cold, so we sat on the grass chattering, disturbed the Spanish campers and caused the man to clap his hands at us

Flamenco-style. We moved onto the football pitch next to the campsite and chatted, dozed and drank.

Distance cycled: 64km

Cumulative distance: 237km

Wednesday 4th September - loop of the Alsace wine route (from Ruffach back to Rouffach)

We were to head today for 'l'un des plus beaux villages de France' - Eguisheim. It wasn't too far away, 13km perhaps, but the route was hilly and all above us. We left our luggage behind but took a picnic which we planned to accompany with wine bought direct from a producer along the way.

We had breakfast at l'Ours Noir near the church, comprising their coffee plus pastries from the boulangerie. Then we got more bread from the boulangerie and a load of picnic foods from the little supermarket - pâté, saucisson, fromages, etc.

Here the place-names looked German but were spelt and pronounced French style. The route was out via Pfaffenheim, Gueberschwihr, Voeglinshoffen, Husseren-les-Châteaux and then into Eguisheim. It was indeed hilly and we made very slow progress (well there was no hurry anyway). It actually did not seem any easier without the luggage, than we imagined it would be with it. The villages were pretty but for a long time we didn't see any open wine outlets.

We were in Alsace, an area of France (capital Strasbourg) that has been constantly fought over and has changed hands many times over many years.

Eguisheim was a victim of its own labelling though. It had many lovely old buildings but it was overwhelmed with gawping tourists and most of the shops sold tourist tat. Despite the almost mediaeval look of the buildings, it had a tourist 'train' like Bournemouth seafront's.

Eguisheim produces Alsace wine of high quality. In May 2013 it was voted the «Village préféré des Français» (Favourite French Village), an annual distinction that passes from town to town throughout France. The village centre receives many tourists, as the Alsace "Wine Route" passes the village. The village is also a member of the *Les Plus Beaux Villages de France* ("The most beautiful villages of France") association. Its 2013 election increased visitation by up to 70%.

We locked the bikes and were just wondering where to buy wine, when two big doors opposite opened as if by magic. It was a sign! In we went. The vintner had an odd manner, first he seemed unsure as to why we came into his cellars at all. He had many pictures and newspaper cuttings on the wall, about his dual lives as a winemaker and as a magician, yet he appeared impatient when asked about the latter. We tasted some wines and chose, but then found none of these were available cold so we bought two we had not tried. This episode wasn't very satisfactory but our picnic in a shady little public courtyard garden just off the main street was a great success and a bit of a tourist attraction in itself.

A walk through the town confirmed our initial impression, that tourism had spoiled the very gem that it came to see. Despite this, we lingered for coffees and later ice creams (including cinnamon-flavour).

For the journey home we chose a less picturesque but flatter route alongside the main road for the most part. We spotted a couple of interesting things on the way; one the Ritter (possibly now Grimmer) chocolate factory another a big supermarket on the outskirts of Rouffach. We bought a disposable barbeque, mackerel, sausages and accompaniments and a pineapple for our evening meal and then continued to the small local supermarket to buy wine. Arriving finally at the campsite, we began to worry and went back to buy another lot of wine. It was from the local producer and at about €8 a bottle, was somewhat cheaper than in the restaurant.

The barbeque got off to a shaky start when the self-lighting-cardboard bit fizzled out except in one corner. But some shaking and tilting sorted it out after a while. Meanwhile, the mackerel fillets had been prepared en papillote with butter and were ready to go on. We borrowed tables and benches from the communal dining area and set up a full field kitchen. With the new salads and bread and beer and wine, plus leftovers from lunch, we soon had a feast for fifty. The mackerel were delicious. Sausages were next and we managed nearly all of them however we couldn't manage the pineapple. Sated, we packed up just before curfew and retired to the sports field to be away from the other campers and continued sipping our wine in a quiet, civilised manner.

    Distance cycled: 22km

    Cumulative distance: 259km)

Thursday 5th September - Rouffach to camping Île de Rhin, nr. Brisach am Rhein, via Colmar

We struck camp, packed the pineapple and headed for breakfast at Clementine's, a place we noticed the day before. It was pleasant enough but seemed costly for what it was although this may just have been because we paid for everything in one go. Then we moved on to the Ritter chocolatier where we were puzzled that there were none of the colourfully- wrapped square bars we were expecting. There were a lot of novelties, chocolate teapots, espresso-makers, cheeseboards, cartoon characters and so on. It turns out this is because it was a different and unconnected Ritter, nothing to do with Ritter Sport. Subsequent research could not find any evidence of a French Ritter but did find a company called Grimmer in the same area, so I cannot elaborate unfortunately.

One of our number had the bright idea of buying his wife a large chocolate medallion for her birthday. It was a lovely creation, detailed and with a bespoke inscription, lovingly wrapped and tied with a bow. A couple of days later, he found a cellophane bag in his pannier that had been out in temperatures of 30C+. The cellophane bag contained a sludgy lump of brown goo which he did take home, placed in the fridge and proudly presented to his long suffering wife. We have no record of the conversation that followed.

While we were stopped in two groups out of sight of each other, wondering how and where to cross the main road onto the flatlands, a man in a white Peugeot stopped unbeckoned, twice, just to explain to each group that there was a bridge over it a kilometre away. How kind!

We dawdled our way mainly on minor rural roads then car-free, alongside an initially dry riverbed through horticultural fields then joined another small waterway complete with a coypu and finally reached Colmar. This was a lovely place, touristy but not overwhelmed with tourists.

Colmar (Alsatian: *Colmer*; German during 1871–1918 and 1940–1945: *Kolmar*) is the third-largest commune in Alsace (after Strasbourg and Mulhouse). The city is renowned for its well-preserved old town, its numerous architectural landmarks and its museums, among which is the Unterlinden Museum which houses the *Isenheim Altarpiece* which was sculpted and painted by, respectively, the Germans Nikolaus of Haguenau and Matthias Grünewald in 1512–1516. Colmar is situated on the Alsatian Wine Route and considers itself to be the "capital of Alsatian wine" (*capitale des vins d'Alsace*).

We parked up in the cathedral square in bright sunshine and headed straight for beer and lunch. The waiter was very concerned that our table wasn't big enough, although we didn't care. Just as the food arrived the next table became free and all was well. We had noticed numbers of young people passing by dressed in bin-liners and after questioning a couple of them we found they were actually meant to be condoms, promoting a safe sex campaign by flogging johnnies for €1.

We decided to walk to Tourist Information to get a town map but by the time we got there we didn't need a map after all as we had already seen the whole town! We popped into the cathedral which was well worth a visit as many French and German churches are.

We pressed on across the Rhine flood plain to the intact citadel of Neuf-Brisach which turned out to be not very picturesque. Neuf-Brisach (German: *Neubreisach*) is a fortified town and was intended to guard the border between France and the Holy Roman Empire and subsequently, the German states. It was built after the Treaty of Ryswick in 1697 that resulted in France losing the town of Breisach, on the opposite bank of the Rhine. The town's name means *New Breisach*. Today the town is a UNESCO World Heritage Site.

We stopped for tea, cakes etc. and subsequently checked that the camping here was open. It was, but we decided to press on to the next camping; campsite Île de Rhin which is on the Île de Rhin, still in France but within easy reach of Breisach am Rhein on the German side. The campsite had free showers, a kaleidoscopic system of make-up mirrors and a chaotic pitch-numbering system. When we arrived, the temperature gauge showed 33C which surprised us. It was hot but we didn't think it was that hot!

We planned to cycle into town but changed our minds and walked, stopping at the first restaurant we came to for a beer called Radler (means cyclist, tastes like shandy? It is shandy!). *Radler* is indeed German for "cyclist" and has a long history in German-speaking regions. It commonly consists of a 50:50 mixture of beer and sparkling lemonade.

The term *Radler* originated with a drink called *Radlermass* ("cyclist liter") that was originally created by innkeeper Franz Kugler in the small town of Deisenhofen, just outside Munich. During the great cycling boom of the Roaring Twenties, Kugler created a bicycle trail from Munich, through the woods, which led directly to his drinking establishment. On a June day in 1922, 13,000 cyclists arrived at Kugler's. Fast running out of beer, he blended it 50:50 with lemon soda!

We also drank wine and ate goulash soup, noodle soup, pork and beef-based mains and Bratkartoffeln (German Pan Fried Potatoes, usually made with bacon and onions). Our waitress turned out to be a Turkish Gastarbeiter. We returned sleepily to bed.

Distance cycled: 41km

Cumulative distance: 300km

Thursday 6th September - Brisach am Rhein, to Bristol

Up reasonably early, we struck camp for the final time, packed the pineapple for the final time and cycled into Breisach with luggage. On the way in there was a rather spectacular ornament - the Kugelbrunnen Neutor, a sphere of pink granite, perhaps a metre in diameter, rotating in a cavity in a larger piece of grey granite apparently due to water springing from underneath it - what an excellent toy. We proceeded to eat an excellent breakfast in the sunshine which included Zwiebelkuche (onion tart) and Apfel or Zwetschensknitte (apple or plum slice). Then we picked up the cycle route to Freiburg, which on the whole was flat and well marked – just one major uphill where we were overtaken by two girls cycling with rucksacks on. Luckily we had already stopped to finally eat the pineapple!

After the hill and a bit of level, we freewheeled luxuriously down into the sleepy town of Waltershofen where we stopped for a well-earned beer at a corner bar. From here we admired the burnished copper down-pipes of the Rathaus (town hall).

Afterwards, we had soon seen the last of the countryside as we headed into the outskirts of Freiburg. Confusion resulted in us arriving in two parties, one at the bike hire, one at the station ticket office. Both places took an inordinate amount of time! The bikes were inspected, one found wanting but then passed fit and we were irritated to be charged €5 per bike for cleaning although possibly we just didn't read the terms.

As the bike office seemed a bit dippy today and as we had not as much time as we had expected, we decided not to leave luggage there but instead to hobble to the restaurant with it. We passed over the 'bike bridge' as we had a week before, slightly surprised by the number of teenagers climbing the superstructure – mostly girls in fact. Returning also to the same Italian restaurant, we were greeted once more in polyglot style and we ate similar food and drank similar beer and the waitress said 'cheers' in all the languages of Europe.

Then it was onto the train straight through to the airport, where some of us had a final wurst and a beer whilst others shopped. On the plane, the hostess was Louisa who was also responsible for delivering our friend on Monday and the cuisine included cold onion bhaji sandwiches - a first and last!

Distance cycled: 24km

Cumulative distance: 324km

Conclusions

As with all our trips, this was a great success. The Black Forest was stunning and taking the train up the hill was a good move resulting in an easy run into Basel.

The route could have been completed in fewer days than we took but we decided to extend west into France and have a day off from cycling by staying in one campsite for two nights.

As usual, we met many wonderful people and ate and drank some great food. Camping is a great way to stay, with picnics for lunch, and the odd barbeque thrown in makes for a great trip.

In 2015, two friends of ours borrowed the maps and guide book and completed the full circuit without the western French section. They aren't keen campers so booked accommodation as they went in Pensions and Gasthouses and had a great trip.

Appendix 1 - a summary of a friend's trip

Following our successful trip, two friends of ours attempted a similar adventure in 2015. They had a slightly different approach in that they didn't do the detour into France and also stayed in guest houses rather than camping.

They used our maps and guide books and hired bikes from Freiburg as we did. This is an abbreviated account which will hopefully give the reader alternative options.

***

Thursday 21 May - Bristol to Freiburg

Having arrived at Frankfurt Airport on a flight from Bristol and retrieved our panniers, we made our way to the railway station for the train to Freiberg.

I had booked a hotel room that, as far as I could understand from the blurb on the web site, was '10 minutes from the Ald Stadt'. Arriving at the hotel and dumping our panniers and barely wasting a minute to liberate a few essentials, we set off to look for a drink and some food.

Realising that the local supermarket was about to shut, we ran around picking up the essentials for a picnic supper including a large bag of pretzels and a bottle of wine and went back to the hotel where we sat outside on our little terrace, serenaded by a blackbird perched on a nearby roof, silhouetted against the fading light of the sky.

***

Friday 22 May - Freiburg to Neubierhausle

We were up promptly for breakfast and to re-organise our panniers, the carefully packed panniers that left Bristol were not so tidy and strangely full. The manageress told us that we can get the tram into Freiburg and helpfully gave us change with the correct coins for the tram. This was lucky as the payment system was not altogether clear but we managed to work it out and bought our tickets from the machine on the tram. The tram was crowded but efficient and within 10 minutes we were standing outside the Hauptbahnhof.

The bike station was next to the rail station. Sorting out the bikes was fairly straightforward, the seat posts were adjusted, the tyres pumped and we were off.

We wobbled through Freiburg and got diverted back into the Ald Stadt where the route went over cobbled streets and through shaded squares full of tables of people enjoying a relaxed late breakfast/mid morning coffee/early lunch but finally we were out of town and riding along the side of the river in sunshine towards Kirchzarten.

When reaching Kirchzarten, we had a choice according to the guide book. Those of a robust constitution could take the 'Variante fur Sportliche', a 25km diversion that the guide book advised as *'Many metres high, but also beautiful viewpoints and healthy nature are your bid on this challenging variant'* or we could get on a train to Hinterzarten at the top of the mountain in front of us. We decided to let the train take the strain.

After getting help from a young woman on how to buy a ticket from a machine (no ticket office of course), we loaded our bikes onto the train and were lifted up 1000m over the hill to Hinterzarten. It seemed a good idea to stop at the bar opposite the station and have our first beer of the day in the sunshine and it seemed an even better idea to follow that with our second beer of the day in the sunshine. We had thought that we might stay that night at Titisee which was only 4km further so no need to rush.

When we got to Titisee we found a resort bustling with holidaymakers which detracted somewhat from the famously serene beauty of the lake. Neither of us fancied staying there so we checked the Lonely Planet guide and spotted somewhere just outside Titisee that sounded appealing.

The Hotel - Pension Neubierhausle was about 4km out of Titisee in the Neustadt direction and run by

Birgit Hermann. We went in to ask for a room and were offered a choice of rooms; one at the back looking over the fields of cows or one at the front looking towards the tree covered mountain peaks. We chose the front one which had a balcony and a 'stylish bathroom with walk in rain shower'.

Birgit brought us tea and cake on the terrace, the cake came with little pots of homemade jam and cream cheese. Chris, Birgit's husband, made all the jams for the hotel and as we found at breakfast, his range is wide (strawberry, cherry, apricot and others). Birgit spoke excellent English and was happy to chat about the area. The hotel had been run by her parents until she and Chris took it over a few years previously so it was very much a family concern; her father and husband were working in the front garden putting up a fence while we lounged on the terrace with our tea.

We bought the makings of another picnic supper from a nearby supermarket and had a very enjoyable evening sitting on the balcony with a bottle of wine and our picnic watching a fox hunt along the field over the road. Chris lent us his binoculars so we could attempt to identify the birds of prey also hunting across the fields.

Distance cycled 19km

Cumulative distance 19km

***

Saturday 23 May - Neubierhausle to Stühlingen

Breakfast was a wonderful feast of local breads, homemade jams and a wide range of meats and cheeses and we made the most of it.

This was followed by a lengthy chat with Birgit about the farming methods that had brought back the wild flowers to the meadows which were just being cut for the first time that year. Birgit had picked a vase of these flowers which was sitting on the hall table and the variety of flowers was most impressive, including scabious, buttercups, clover and ox eye daisies.

Our bill for all this luxury was €67.20 which seemed ridiculously cheap but apparently we got a €12 discount for having the Lonely Planet book!

As a result of all this, we did not get back in the saddle until 11:30 so not an early start.

But the sun was shining and the road beckoned and we set off with a vague plan that we would stop at Bonndorf for the night.

We re-joined the cycle route at Neustadt and carried on beside the river Gutach on a forest trail. This meant that the surface was a mix of gravel and cinders so OK but a bit stony in places. We had a lot of that over the course of the day.

Early on we came across two women who had stopped beside the track so, minding my manners, I asked if everything was OK with them. They said they were fine so we continued, never expecting to see them again. Little did we know then that we had just met the women who would become our guardian angels.

The trail meandered through the forest and we were treated to views across the valley as well as fields of purple orchids and lupins ranging from pale blue to deepest royal blue. After an enjoyable downhill whizz, we arrived at Lenzkirch and as it was 12:30 it seemed a good idea to stop at the first bar we came to and have a beer in the sunshine.

We decided that one beer was enough today and pressed on up the other side of the valley. The route started to get a bit hilly after that and so more effort was required especially when it reverted to forest trail and cinder surface under wheels.

We emerged from the forest into daylight at about 16:00 when we were above Bonndorf. I was quite tired by then as I had found the forest trails hard work so in theory, I was keen that we stuck to our original plan that Bonndorf was our target for the day. But as we cycled into the small town, we both agreed that it was singularly unappealing, it was completely deserted and not very attractive. According to the guide book, the route would shortly drop down 450m to Stühlingen so we decided to head for there.

Somehow, we missed the route markings and were riding out of Bonndorf, very fast but on a road that did not appear to be bike-friendly. Luckily we realised we must have gone wrong before the return journey was too long or too steep. Back in Bonndorf, we found that we were not the only ones to have got lost, there were several small groups of cyclists circling the streets, like wasps round a jam pot, looking anxiously for that wretched little green man on a bike.

I eventually spotted the sneaky sign post hidden behind some vegetation and all four of us set off again across a flat patchwork of fields of dark green early wheat and brilliant yellow rape.

The route was now on the road so the going was easier and it got a lot easier when we started to go downhill for about 11km. We whistled through Lausheim and Grimmelshofen (both places that I had earmarked as possible alternatives to Bonndorf but both of which were smaller and more deserted if that was possible) at great speed and then when the road levelled off, the route switched back onto a cinder track through more fields of wild flowers.

Just outside Stühlingen, my bike got a puncture in the front wheel. I was not pleased but decided as we were so close to our destination, I would walk the bike into town and work out how to fix it once we had found a hotel and a beer. As we walked along the path, the two women we had passed in the morning caught up with us and noticed the flat tyre. They asked whether we were OK and where we were going. On hearing that we were going to look for accommodation in Stühlingen, they looked a bit worried and said that they hoped we would find somewhere. They were stopping in Stühlingen and maybe we could follow them to their hotel (pre-booked of course) and there might be a room available for us? I said that they were not to wait for us, we'd be fine.

At the first bar in Stühlingen, we parked up and I ordered a beer. My friend generously offered to ride into town and scout out the accommodation options as well as the location of the nearest bike shop. I had already figured that fixing the puncture might be a bit tricky as the wheel was firmly attached to the frame with a bolt, not a quick release lever and of course my limited tool kit did not include a spanner. The beer worked a treat in allaying my concerns about the lack of spanner; how difficult could it be to fix a puncture, after all?

Then she returned with some bad news; there was not a room to be had in this town or even the next town and the local camp site would not let us in without a tent. A small detail which we had overlooked was that this weekend was a Bank Holiday in Germany and Germans take their holidays very seriously. This explained why everywhere was so deserted - and closed - and why our fellow travellers had looked worried when we said we did not have accommodation booked. She had spotted the local bike shop which was only a few yards along the road; and shut until Tuesday.

The bench on the pavement began to look as if it might become 'home' for the next few nights.

However, we struck gold in selecting the hotel in which to make initial enquiries as, after the manageress had phoned round and established that everywhere was full, she took pity on us and said we could have her room in the hotel and she would sleep elsewhere and her son would fix the puncture overnight.

Once we had got ourselves into the room (very small single room with a foldaway bed squeezed in), we decided that it would be good form to have supper in the hotel restaurant. Well, it was that or no supper at all as we had only half a packet of pretzels left and no shops were open.

As luck would have it, the two women cyclists (Regina and Beate) were also in the restaurant; it turned out that this was where they had booked a room. We got chatting and they explained about the Bank Holiday and that they were doing two thirds of the route whilst their husbands were doing the whole route and they were meeting up with them on Monday near Basel. They had expected a friend to join them but she had developed a knee problem so had been unable to come. This meant that they had a room for three in the hotel and more interestingly, a room for four in Bad Säckingen and did we want to share it with them?

It must have taken us less than 10 seconds to agree that this was a fine idea and as long as they did not mind sharing with us, we would be more than delighted to share with them.

I hoped that the offer would still be open when the benevolent effects of the wine had worn off overnight.

Distance cycled 50km

Cumulative distance 69km

***

Sunday 24 May - Stühlingen to Bad Säckingen

After a good night's sleep; the foldaway bed was way more comfortable than any park bench, we trotted downstairs for breakfast. Our saintly hostess, Christine, said that she had slept on the office floor as that was better than attempting to share a room with her husband who was a loud snorer. We did feel a trifle guilty about this.

Luckily, Regina and Beate reiterated their offer to share the room in Bad Säckingen and we agreed that we would meet them there that evening. They set off and we gave them a 10 minute head start before following them out of Stühlingen.

The route followed an easy path alongside the river and we planned to stop for lunch at Waldshut. Looking at the map, it seemed likely that there would be a number of places along the path where there would be pubs or at least small shops where we could buy some food so we decided to pass on Waldshut. It was surprising to find that everything was shut; garden centres that in England would be bustling with families buying their summer bedding plants were quiet as graveyards and even the big supermarkets (Lidl, Aldi as well as the local ones) were all decidedly closed.

At times, the route took us through strange deserted suburbs, all neat houses and even neater front gardens but not a soul to be seen. It was as if a bomb had been dropped that removed all signs of human life but left the buildings intact. Quite spooky.

Eventually we stopped in a field on the outskirts of some suburb or other where we polished off the remains of the remains of yesterday's picnic so that would be a couple of tomatoes, a dried hunk of bread and more of those pretzels that seemed to be self replenishing. It was hardly a feast but filled a gap.

Then we arrived in Laufenberg and found people again, in fact a small town bustling with life and ice creams and kids riding bikes. Gratefully, we parked our bikes beside a table outside a Greek bar and ordered a couple of beers. The Rhine was flowing by, wide and thick and fast with small river cruisers ploughing their way up and down stream filled with happy tourists. There was a bridge over the river with Switzerland on the other side and as we swallowed the first cold welcome draft of beer, the clock in the church tower on the Swiss side was striking three o'clock.

About half an hour later, Regina and Beate turned up on their bikes. They pedalled over the bridge to pay a quick visit to Switzerland and on their way back, spotted us sitting with our beers. They had stopped at Waldshut and had lunch; apparently it is a pretty medieval town with lovely views and well worth a visit. Ah well, next time maybe.

They left us to our beers and then we followed them on towards Bad Säckingen. The last few kilometres to our destination we were on a path that ran along the land side of a number of 'posh allotments'. Each plot was a good size and had been lovingly cared for with orchards and vegetable plots and tucked close to the river, summer houses where whole families were engaged in barbeques. We decided that this was where all the people must be that plainly weren't in the suburbs.

Arriving in Bad Säckingen, we made our way to the Munsterplatz which was laid out with numerous tables filled with people eating and drinking. It was time for tea and cake!

After our tea, we headed for the Gasthaus Hallwyer Hof which, to our delight, was right on the river next to the amazing Holzbrücke (wooden bridge) over the Rhine to Switzerland.

Regina and Beate had booked the 4 bed room which had its own bathroom and dining room and was minimalist and bright and white with polished wooden floors throughout and a view across the Rhine to Switzerland via the bridge.

The covered bridge spans 203.7m (668ft) over the Rhine and is the longest roofed wooden bridge in Europe. The boundary line between Switzerland and Germany in the middle is marked by a prominent yellow plaque decorated with the Bundesrepublick Eagle. So no lingering doubts as to where you are, then.

That evening, the four of us went for supper at a restaurant in the old streets and as suggested by Regina and Beate, had Flammeküche, a local speciality. Apparently this was not the best version of the dish but it was close enough, a bit like a pizza with additional calories in the form of lots of fromage blanc, sautéed onions and lardons. After a lot of chat, the evening finished with a stroll over the Holzbrücke and back.

Distance cycled 55km

Cumulative distance 124km

***

Monday 25 May - Bad Säckingen to Weil (via Basel)

Although the Bank Holiday was almost over, Regina and Beate were worried that we might have a problem finding accommodation that night so they made a reservation for us at an hotel in Weil am Rhein where their husbands had stayed on the first night of their tour. Then we assembled our rainbow collection of red, blue, yellow and green Ortlieb panniers, loaded the bikes, wished each other good journey and said we would no doubt pass each other several times during the day etc and off Regina and Beate peddled. They were due to meet the husbands later in the day, somewhere along the route. We decided it was time for a coffee at a cafe and a bit of people watching before we set off.

The first part of the route meandered along the side of the river and passed through a nature reserve where there were a lot of men lurking in bushes with enormous telescopes through which they were peering at various birds; we stopped to watch a pair of grebes trying to build a nest as well as swans and herons and a multitude of different types of ducks.

The route got less scenic especially after we crossed the Rhine over a bridge over a dam and passed to Rheinfelden. The town was quite pretty and we re-crossed the river in the town and looked at the defunct customs house then back to the Swiss side.

Eventually, we arrived in the centre of Basel and then our navigation skills really did get a testing. The hotel was in Weil am Rhein which is not shown explicitly on the maps in the guide book though, obviously, it is on the proper map. So, standing by a bridge in Basel with the little green man sign pointing to the left, we decide to go off piste and cross the bridge into Germany and figure out our way to Weil from there. This was not one of our better decisions.

On the other side, there are plenty of cycle route signs including those for the long distance routes such as EuroVelo 5 Via Romea Francigena, EuroVelo 6 Atlantic to Black Sea and EuroVelo 15 Rhine route and several seemed to indicate the Weil might be on them but after we had ridden round in a circle we came to rest back by the river, got out the pretzel bag and maps and compass and did some serious scratching of heads.

Things got worse after that; with hindsight and in the comfort of home, it is obvious that we should have kept the faith and followed the little green man signs and we would have arrived at our hotel in less than an hour after reaching the centre of Basel. Instead we had the opportunity to cycle round in circles in several places that purported to be Weil but were not the bit of Weil that we were looking for and we got a lot of practice in asking directions from a varied range of people.

Eventually, we arrived at the Hotel Dreiländereck and were welcomed by the smell of the Chinese restaurant on the ground floor which permeated upwards to the room but it was perfectly clean and the bikes were locked into a garage.

We decided that we were not in the mood for a Chinese meal so we wandered along the road for a few metres to a Turkish restaurant that was buzzing. We had two beers sitting at the pavement tables then decided to go inside and eat and I had the best Turkish food ever from the friendliest Turkish waiters and we ended the day feeling very full and happy.

Distance cycled 52km

Cumulative distance 176km

***

Tuesday 26 May - Weil am Rhein to Heitersheim

We were keen to leave Weil but not so keen that we managed an early start. The night had been disturbed by carousing on the streets at odd times, I suppose it was the end of the Bank Holiday and I think there was a football match involved.

After breakfast, we wandered down the street and stocked up on the essentials for the day, mainly bread, pate, tomatoes, lettuce and of course another large bag of pretzels. You just never know when a pretzel moment will arrive.

My friend was sitting outside the hotel while I wandered off to take a picture of the Turkish restaurant (easier than writing its name in a notebook) and when I returned, I found her talking to Regina and Beate and their husbands. They had met up the previous day and had stayed the night in a hotel just a 100m further down the street. Apparently, they had been taking shelter from the rain in a McDonald's somewhere outside Basel and saw us peddling on regardless (we didn't mention the 3 hours it had taken to find the hotel as it might have seemed a tad churlish since they had booked it for us). The husbands were charming and said that they had heard all about us, I didn't ask for particulars but it sounded as if we had left a positive impression on Regina and Beate.

One of them explained how to get back on the route (straight up the road, turn left, you can't miss it, then along the side of the river which needs to be flowing to our right, if it is flowing to the left, we were going in the wrong direction!). They were going to cycle to Basel (a short journey for some) and get the train back to north Germany where they came from.

After much hugging and good wishes, they departed and we got ready to saddle up and get back on the route. Needless to say, we managed to miss the left turn and cycled up a steepish hill back to one of the other Weils that we had visited the day before. Somewhat irritated, we retraced our path and found the correct left turn and then we were off out of Weil.

The clouds were still around and there was the occasional shower but mainly it was just a bit dull. The route became cinder track again and followed the river edge.

We decided to go into Bad Bellingen for lunch and hopefully, a beer. It was a very strange place indeed. The first hotel bar we came across was closed so we cycled further and found lots of posh hotels but with no-one around; ghost town again. We found the centre (maybe) but all that was there was a small bakery so we bought two bottles of Coca Cola and sat on the bench eating our meagre picnic and watching a woman prune a shrub, one twig at a time. No doubt that counted as an exciting activity in Bad Bellingen.

Eventually we reached Neuenburg where the route turned inland. It was good to be out in the open again and we peddled along a path beside flat fields that stretched away on either side of us. We were approaching Heitersheim and thought we would stop there for the night. So first thing was to find the Tourist Information office which is usually located in the Rathaus but by the time we had located the place, it was closed for the day, it was only just after 16:00 but plainly they were not expecting visitors.

So we went to the first hotel we passed and booked a room there. It was not very appealing but it was available, large and had a balcony so it would do. In theory, we wanted to stay somewhere for two nights so that we could explore the neighbouring villages without our panniers but we decided that Heitersheim was not the place. It was another ghost town, all very clean but without people or any sense of life. We had a beer sitting outside a bar and fed the sparrows with some pretzel crumbs which they seemed to enjoy. Then we got some food from a supermarket and went back to our balcony to eat it and turn in for an early night.

Distance cycled 43km

Cumulative distance 219km

***

Wednesday 27 May - Heitersheim to Kirchhofen

We decided to make an early start with the Tourist Information office and see if we could book our train tickets from Freiburg to Frankfurt in advance and save some money. Unfortunately it seemed the Tourist Information office cannot book train tickets or tell us anything about anywhere other than Heitersheim. We knew that we were not far from Freiburg so decided to carry on the general direction and see what we could find of interest on the way.

We spotted a sign to the Malteserschloss so we decided to visit it. It had a lovely garden around it and a very cool looking cafe so, since we had cycled about 3km, it was time to stop for a coffee. By now, the sun had returned and the temperature was rising and we had a pleasant hour looking at the view.

We cycled another few kilometres to Bad Krozingen which had a railway station so we headed there and parked up outside. I stayed to guard the bikes and soak up the sunshine while my friend went inside to do battle with the ticket booking system.

We reached Kirchhofen and found the hotel Ambringer Bad easily and the hotel was the first building on the edge of the village. But strangely, the place looked very closed and no-one came to the door in response to our knocking.

Undeterred, we rearranged the garden furniture and settled down for our picnic accompanied by a cold bottle of beer each that we had bought from a small shop. Every 15 minutes or so, one of us would go and knock on the door again to no avail. Then we decided to call the place and that worked a treat. Moments later, the manageress opened the door and showed us to our room. No comment was made about the rearranged garden furniture.

It had been suggested to us we should visit Staufen which was about 4km from Kirchhofen so once we had dumped the panniers, we cycled off to Staufen. As promised, it was a very pretty little town with old timbered buildings and a castle on the hill. There were signs for the path up to the castle but we decided that it was time for tea and cake so made our way to the Ratplatz and slumped in the sun stuffing our faces with an enormous walnut and maple syrup sundae and a slice of rhubarb tart cake.

After the tea, we went for a ride around the town taking in the sights and a beer back in the Ratplatz, before cycling back to Kirchhofen. The sun was getting lower in the sky and there were shadows now in the fields, parallel lines where the young sweetcorn was pushing upwards and the cabbages were sprouting. The hedgerows were stuffed with mock orange (*philadelphus*) bushes but strangely, none of them seemed to have any scent.

Kirchhofen seemed deserted apart from a few boys riding round the village pond and shouting at each other so we decided to hunker down in our room and read for a few hours. A peaceful night followed.

Distance cycled 22km

Cumulative distance 241km

***

Thursday 28 May - Kirchhofen to Freiburg

After breakfast which was fine but far from spectacular, we set off on the last leg, a very short leg of about 15km to central Freiburg. The plan was to arrive in town around midday, sort out a place to stay, dump our panniers and spend the rest of the day doing a spot of gentle sightseeing, maybe a few beers, followed by tea and cake and wrap up with a blow-out dinner. What could possibly go wrong?

The route was pretty straightforward wending its way through some gently hilly vineyards before cruising into the suburbs of Freiburg.

By 11:00 we were passing an ice cream parlour which seemed very popular with the locals so we stopped for a coffee. My friend had opened the Lonely Planet and was considering our accommodation options. We wanted to be in central Freiburg but we did not want to spend mega bucks on a fancy hotel so the Lonely Planet suggested the Black Forest Hostel.

To quote 'The Black Forest Hostel offers beds for a good value in dormitories as well as in double and single rooms. The hostel is located near the historic part of Freiburg and it is easy to reach.' I was a bit worried about the 'good value in dormitories' and hoped that the dormitories were fully booked. But first we had to find the place and I took issue with the 'easy to reach' statement.

First impressions were not good as we walked into Reception, we were met by an overwhelming smell of disinfectant. As we had not come with our own bedding we had to 'rent' duvets, pillows, sheets, pillow cases and duvet covers, towels were not on offer so it was lucky that we had our own, unused up until now, in our panniers. Worse, it was self catering so no breakfast!

But I was being unduly pessimistic; we were shown to a room with three beds and the bathrooms, clearly marked with a picture of a Man and a Woman, were just outside our room and the rented sheets were squeaky clean and ironed.

We dumped our panniers and set off to explore the uneven delights of Freiburg and it was lovely. A really attractive old town with a fabulous market spread across the Munsterplatz with many bars serving beer, strangely enough. We wandered around and admired the street paving and the trams and the hundreds of cyclists, had a brilliant tea and cake (rhubarb cake and apricot cheesecake), a few beers in the sunshine and then in the evening we walked into the old town and found a lively restaurant by the stream that runs through. We had a fantastic meal; trout and spatzle with a good bottle of wine.

Distance cycled 15km

Cumulative distance 256km

***

Day 9 – Friday 29 May - Freiburg to Bristol

As breakfast had to be foraged, we were up, packed, bedding dragged back down to Reception, passports retrieved and out of the door by 09.00 and circling round a rather sleepy town looking for an appealing café.

Following breakfast sitting outside under the awning, we went back to the market in Munsterplatz to buy some mementos of our visit to Germany, we wanted mountain cheese and Black Forest ham and sausages and we found all of these. Had we been staying for longer, we would have stocked up on a lot more as the range and variety of fresh produce was mouth wateringly wonderful. The buckets of flowers were a kaleidoscope of colours and perfumes.

We then returned to the bike rental station, it was hard to believe that it had only been a week ago when we were picking up the bikes and the trip was all ahead of us.

After that, it was back on the train to Frankfurt and then the plane to Bristol.

Distance cycled 4km

Cumulative distance 260km/163 miles)

Cycling the Weser-Radweg - Hann. Münden to Minden

"I thought of that while riding my bicycle" - Albert Einstein on discovering the theory of relativity

Introduction

In the new year, thoughts usually turn to where and we'd like to cycle in that year. This can take a while, this trip was decided upon reasonably quickly. We'd had a river trip in Germany before along part of the Elbe and had hired decent bikes. We had been to France on five previous occasions and had enjoyed our two previous trips to Germany so decided to give Germany a go once more.

Germany is a big country with a lot of scope for cycling. The Germans have many way marked cycle routes including many along rivers i.e. the Elbe, Rhine and Danube. A bit of internet research found the river Weser and its cycleway the Weser Radweg.

We needed to get there fairly easily from Bristol and decided upon a BMI flight to Hamburg, to hire bikes and take a train to the start of the Radweg in Hann. Münden.

What were we about to attempt?

The river Weser has its source at Hannoversch Münden formed by the confluence of the rivers Fulda and Werra. The Weser flows through Lower Saxony, then reaches Bremen, before emptying into the North Sea 50km further north at Bremerhaven. On the opposite (west) bank is the town of Nordenham at the foot of the Butjadingen Peninsula; thus, the mouth of the river is in Lower Saxony. The Weser has an overall length of 452km. Together with its Werra tributary, which originates in Thuringia, its length is 744km.

The Weser cycle path is a 520km long-distance cycle route, which was awarded the ADFC 4-star quality cycle route in 2017. In the 2016 ADFC cycle travel analysis, the Weser cycle path was recognized as Germany's second most popular cycle route.

Well-known cities along the Weser and on the bike path are Hann. Münden, Höxter, Holzminden, Bodenwerder, Hameln, Rinteln, Bad Oeynhausen, Minden, Petershagen, Nienburg, Verden, Bremen, Brake, Nordenham, Bremerhaven and Cuxhaven.
The Weser can be crossed by ferries in many places.

It takes the rider through 8 regions in eight stages: Hann. Münden to Höxter; Höxter to Hameln; Hameln to Minden; Minden to Nienburg; Nienburg to Verden;

Verden to Bremen; Bremen to Nordenham / Bremerhaven and Bremerhaven to Cuxhaven

The Weser cycle path is part of the cycle network Germany, a national cycle route network of twelve national cycle routes and is part of D-Route 9 *Weser - Romantic Road.*

The Weser cycle path begins at the source of the Weser near Hann. Münden and follows the course of the river to its mouth in the North Sea at Bremerhaven. From there it continues to Cuxhaven and meets the Elbe Cycle Path. The length of the bike path exceeds the 452 river kilometres by around 50km because it cannot always exactly follow the course of the river. In large parts, bike paths are available on both sides of the river, so that there are almost always alternative sections in addition to the official main route.

It's a very easy cycle as the height difference between Hann. Münden and Minden is small (75m in 199km) and that between Porta Westfalica and the North Sea coast is even less (40m in over 250 river kilometres). The surfaces are excellent, easily completed on road, hybrid or touring bikes.

The Weser cycle path (Weser-Radweg) is crossed by several railway lines, which provide good access to the cycle path in Hann. Münden, Bad Karlshafen, Höxter and Holzminden. From Hameln, railway lines run parallel to the Weser via Bad Oeynhausen (Weserbahn), Minden, Nienburg, Verden to Bremen.

***

Our plan was to start at Hann. Münden and go as far north as we could in the time before our flight home. As there were many places we could find a train, this was fairly straightforward. Navigation is easy, following the signs for the Weser-Radweg (a stylised bike with the words "WESER-RADWEG" and "Vom Weserbergland bis zur Nordsee"). We also took the excellent Bikeline book "Weser-Radweg: Von Hann. Münden nach Cuxhaven", although in German it had excellent 1:50,000 maps and showed where there were campsites along the route. We usually don't book campsites in advance, especially in France i.e. the Loire, Bordeaux and Montpellier trips for instance as we were going to touristy areas and we knew we would have plenty of choice. On this trip we did book in advance because campsites were fewer and we wanted to ensure we could get a pitch. It also meant we had a hard target at the end of each day and had something to aim for. This was good and bad, we couldn't easily shorten the day or maybe it would mean we had one or two fewer stops. It also meant we cycled more than we had done on other trips did but the cycling was very easy.

***

We had flown with bikes on a pervious trip (river Elbe in 2011) and have taken bikes on ferries to France. We've also successfully hired bikes in Germany (Black forest trip in 2013) and in France. The river Weser area is not difficult to get to but time consuming by ferry and train and the BMI plane from Bristol to Hamburg (the nearest airport to the area) had planes too small to take bikes so hiring it was then.

Internet research found a couple of likely hire shops but we settled on Hamburg City Cycles in Bernhard Nocht Strasse. Their main focus is in guided bike tours of the city but do offer bikes for hire so we plumped for the "trekking bike" option, good, solid 8-speed bikes with pannier racks and mudguards (we brought our own bottle cages), locks, tools, spare tubes and helmets were also included.

That's it, we were good to go!

Friday 15 June - Bristol to Hamburg

We all met at Bristol Airport for the BMI flight to Hamburg and each placed a pannier and a tent into one of two large bags to go in the hold with the other pannier as hand luggage. We had flown with BMI before but to Frankfurt on the 2013 Black Forest trip. On that trip, we wondered how an airline flying small planes which were rarely full could survive. On this trip we were about to find out!

Everything was very civilised, all on time and we arrived at Hamburg airport on time. Hamburg Airport is like any other and after considering a couple of options we spotted a taxi large enough to take us into town.

We had booked the Hotel Meininger in the Goetheallee area of Hamburg and were checked in by the delightful Hannah, who also advised on nearby eating places, including a street festival and a 'traditional German' restaurant. The Meininger was well chosen, in a central position, a short walk from Altona railway station and it had a bar and promised an all-you-can-eat-breakfast the next morning.

Our communal room was stylish and clean and even had a separate private shower and WC room.

After settling in, we had a beer in the Meininger bar then wandered off and soon found the street festival, the music seemed to be over but thankfully there were still *Würsten* to be had, and some of us availed ourselves of a *Krakower* sausage just as a sharpener. It then seemed to be a bit difficult to find anywhere still serving food, so when we did, we jumped in. It may, or may not, have been the 'traditional German' restaurant mentioned by Hannah, but it was quite nice anyway. When we attempted to pay we found they wouldn't take payment cards, except German ones. This was to be a bit of a theme during the trip, we never did find out why.

Distance cycled: 0km

Cumulative distance: 0km)

Saturday 16 June - Hamburg to Hann. Münden

We availed ourselves thoroughly of the all-you-can-eat breakfast in the hostel, which was pretty comprehensive. The place was busy, patrons included German families playing at shooting each other with imaginary handguns and hung over British youths having had a night out on the nearby Reeperbahn (street and entertainment district, one of the two centres of Hamburg's nightlife and also the city's major red-light district - it is nicknamed *die sündigste Meile* (the most sinful mile)) not to mention a very civilised cycling group comprising British retirees.

As in most of our trips, we visit large, and/or interesting cities but don't always have much time to explore, the purpose of the trip is to cycle and extra days on at the beginning or end would either extend the trip or eat into the cycling time. I'd never been to Hamburg (apart from passing through it on a train many years ago) and it did look like a decent place to spend some time.

Hamburg officially the Free and Hanseatic City of Hamburg (*Freie und Hansestadt Hamburg)* is the second-largest city in Germany after Berlin with a population of over 1.84 million.

One of Germany's 16 federal states, it is surrounded by Schleswig-Holstein to the north and Lower Saxony to the south. The city's metropolitan region is home to more than five million people. Hamburg lies on the River Elbe and two of its tributaries, the River Alster and the River Bille.

Hamburg is Europe's third-largest port. The city is a major international and domestic tourist destination. It ranked 18th in the world for livability in 2016.

After checkout we strolled the few hundred metres to Altona Station on the S-Bahn and were soon on board for the three stations to Stadthausbrücke down by the harbour. It was then a short few hundred yard walk to Hamburg City Cycles. It was very busy there, bikes coming and going, and there was also filming in progress down the road, where a car repeatedly drove through a police roadblock causing an officer to jump out of the way.

After waiting until the day hirers had been given their bikes we got our steeds, adjusted them, loaded our luggage, left our air-travel bags in the shop and set off across town along a sightseeing route.

We passed many landmarks including the Bismarck Monument (The Bismarck Monument (*Bismarck-Denkmal*) a memorial dedicated to Otto von Bismarck and probably best-known of these Bismarck towers) and St. Michael's church.

We stopped for a look at the ruined tower of St. Nikolai. The Church of St. Nicholas (*St.-Nikolai-Kirche*) is a Gothic Revival cathedral that was formerly one of the five Lutheran *Hauptkirchen* (main churches) in Hamburg. The original chapel, a wood building, was completed in 1195. It was replaced by a brick church in the 14th century, which was eventually destroyed by fire in 1842. The church was completely rebuilt by 1874 and was the tallest building in the world from 1874 to 1876.

The bombing of Hamburg in World War II destroyed the bulk of the church. The removal of the rubble left only its crypt, its site and tall-spired tower, largely hollow save for a large set of bells. These ruins continue to serve as a memorial and an important architectural landmark. The remains of the old church are the second-tallest structure in Hamburg. In 2005, a lift was installed to a 75metre-high platform. The tower and some remains of the wall have since been preserved as a memorial against war.

Then past the Rathaus and the Binnenalster and Außenalster ornamental lakes.

Hauptbahnhof Hamburg was very busy and there were a lot of cyclists trying to use the limited lifts, we were conscious of trying to stay together as we were travelling on a single ticket - although the bikes had a ticket each for some reason. A last-minute platform change (worthy of Birmingham New Street) split us and forced us to use escalators, illegally. But we were reunited on the train thankfully.

The train journey was five hours long and involved changes at Uelzen and Göttingen, so we had plenty of time to chat, doze, read, stare out of the windows and charge phones.

Finally we arrived in Hann. Münden, we decided to ignore the purist entreaties and skipped the very first bit of the true route and coasted a 1km shortcut downhill to the riverside campsite - Campingplatz Hann. Münden. We were told to pitch anywhere in a large field by the river and below a road viaduct. There were only a handful of other tent campers, some of whom had canoes, some kayaks and some bikes. "Too much choice', but we duly placed ourselves in a small British defensive circle miles from the others (but pretty much under the bridge).

Hann. Münden (short for Hannoversch Münden) is in Lower Saxony and is at the confluence of the Fulda and Werra rivers, which join to form the Weser. It is most noted for its half-timbered houses, some of them more than 600 years old.

The town's name means "confluence" in old German; the prefix *Hannoversch*, or "Hanoverian", was added in the 19th century to help distinguish the town from its similarly-named Prussian neighbour, Minden.

The town was indeed very historical looking and had a 42m lead shot tower - Der Hampesche Turm built in 1848 - unfortunately closed to the public. We walked to the square and immediately chose to eat there in an alfresco space. The waitress agreed to keep us a table for about 20 minutes' time, so we went for a beer, which proved a very slow process. Returning to the first restaurant and acquiring a new waitress, we were addressed in French, no matter what we said. It turned out the first one had told her we were French… after clarification she spoke good English and we replied in awful French (/ German / Italian / Spanish).

Distance cycled: 4km

Cumulative distance: 4km

Sunday 17th June Hann. Münden to Bad Karlshafen
(Bikeline Guide §1 to §7)

At last! We set off on the cycling holiday proper... but after a draining 0.5km it was time for breakfast (a surfeit of cake-like things) in the same square as we had dinner in - Ziegelstraße - accompanied now by bells from St Blasius church.

Eventually we set off for a second time towards our destination of Bad Karlshafen. The cycling was easy, almost completely flat barring the odd very small lump. We were following the signs for the Weser Radweg which mostly meant we were on the small L561 on the east (right) bank cycling through farmland of mixed crops. Our day took us from Hann. Münden via Oberweser and Bodenfelde to Bad Karlshafen.

After about 12km, we stopped for coffee in the delightful town of Hemeln and then cycled past the Bursfelde monastery to Oberweser.

More lovely cycling in beautiful weather took us to Bodenfelde where we decided to break for lunch. The route followed the river and wound along rather than taking the most direct route but it was easy cycling and easy navigation.

Along the way we spotted an Archimedes' Screw raising irrigation water and also a commemorative plaque to the reunification of Germany – a process that culminated in 'German Unity Day', 3rd October 1990.

After Bodenfelde, we came off the L561 and onto more rural roads, footpaths and towpaths finally coasting into the baroque town of Bad Karlshafen.

Built by Landgrave Carl zu Hessen around 1700, Bad Karlshafen is considered one of the pearls of the Weserbergland. Bad Karlshafen, also known as "City of Sole Springs" is located at the confluence of the Diemel and the Weser. It claims to have all the facilities of a modern spa and holiday resort with highlights including the German Huguenot Museum, town hall and the harbour. Apparently (and we may have visited it if we had known in advance!) there's a French style Weser-Therme where weary cyclists can visit the "boat sauna - Jacques Galland". The boat apparently gives you the opportunity to completely relax in light waves and a temperature of 85C.

Towards the end of the day, one of us finds he's having a troublesome right pedal which eventually seizes.

The Bad Karlshafen campsite (Camping Bad Karlshafen) came into view sooner than we were expecting - because it is so ginormus - and is situated on a bend in the river in the middle of the town. We checked in and being in small tents, we were told to pitch along the river front, on the flood plain in fact, but it looked safe and we had a lovely view of the river and the town opposite. The eponymous harbour lay across from us but had been drained for repairs, the entrance was dammed and the drainage pumps were driving a sonorous waterfall.

We were cycling during the 2018 Russian-hosted World Cup (cycling during football competitions seems to be a bit of an unplanned habit of ours!) That day, Germany were playing Mexico in a Group F match.

As we were guests in Germany and the campsite had a bar which was showing the match we joined our German friends in a flag festooned bar, drank beer with them and were given free snacks. All our fellow football watchers were on good form and we managed to converse in English and German during the match. Unfortunately, it was a disastrous start to the World Cup campaign for Germany and they contrived to lose 1 - 0. Total silence ensued.

After a couple of beers, plenty of free snacks and after commiserating with our new friends, we returned to our tents where the German resident of the campervan parked behind our tents, was very friendly and interested in our journey.

Bad Karlshafen as a town turned out to be picturesque but largely shut (it was a Sunday after all!). We somehow found the only place open for food – it was a Tardis-like hotel and of course quite popular. We ate a good meal in a small courtyard, by the time we had finished this hotel too was shut.

Distance cycled: 46km

Cumulative distance: 50km

Monday 18th June Bad Karlshafen to Polle
(Bikeline Guide §7 to §12)

We were awoken by bells from the church on the opposite bank to find our camp had been invaded by ducks, presumably looking for discarded breakfast scraps. Out of luck in our case. The German resident of the campervan behind was very friendly and tried to help with the broken pedal, we were very envious of his miniature cycling-sized socket set, but the pedal proved to be unfixable.

We struck camp and headed into town in search of a bike shop. Having asked a couple of locals we were directed to a petrol station (Henrik Ulbricht) with the promise there was a bike shop right next door. Sure enough, next door was Weserberglandbiking on Mündener Str. and a charming young lad sold us and fitted a new pair of pedals for the faulty bike.

We adjourned for a first breakfast, one of us inadvertently chose a bap stuffed with raw meat and onions, this would not again be his first choice for breakfast. The rest of us had better luck with the strawberry and custard tart.

Our day was another pleasant cycle leaving Bad Karlshafen and through Beverungen to Fürstenberg, Höxter, then to Holzminden our lunch venue.

After about 10km of pleasant pedalling along the riverside, we rolled into the charming town of

Beverungen. Leaving over the bridge, we crossed onto the right bank for another 10km along the L550 into Fürstenberg which boasts the Fürstenberg China Factory. Founded in 1747 it is the third-oldest porcelain manufacturer in Germany.

About 7km further on, we re-crossed the river to the west and entered Höxter. Another lovely town combining picturesque half-timbered houses and medieval streets with a lively inner city where we stopped for a mooch round and a coffee.

We didn't visit but a local must see just east and north of Höxter is the UNESCO World Heritage Site of Corvey. The castle and former monastery is a cultural monument, museum and venue regional cultural centre.

Eventually we cycled on about 10km into Holzminden, also known as "City of Fragrances and Flavours" because the (apparently!) well-known fragrance manufacturer Symrise has its headquarters in Holzminden. Apparently we could "discover the sights of the city with a nose" during a fragrant city tour.

Instead, we locked the bikes to a planter and paused for lunch at the *Hafenbar* on Steinhof. We sat outside right on the riverside with an excellent view. The waitress was wearing a Fitbit and explained that she had to walk some way from the kitchen to our table so liked to know how far she had walked.

Returning to the bikes we found there was a duck nesting in the planter, but we managed to disengage the bikes without frightening her off. As we left the town we found that some of the pedestrians along the route, were actually life sized statues. We bumped into the helpful German camper van man again who wished us well.

We had a choice to make on which side of the Weser we would cycle, as the Radweg takes you on either bank at this point, both about 13km to Polle. We opted for right (left was along the small but busier B83).

When we reached Polle the campsite - Campingplatz Weserterrasse - was in a very beautiful setting, on the left bank of the Weser below the castle. We had to cross the river via a small reaction ferry - Gierseilfähre Polle

We had come across reaction ferries on the Elbe trip. A reaction ferry uses the power of the river to tack across the current rather than a powered cable ferry, which uses an engine or electric motors.

A reaction ferry uses the reaction of the current of a river against a fixed tether to propel the vessel across the water. Such ferries operate faster and more effectively in rivers with strong currents.

Some reaction ferries operate using an overhead cable suspended from towers anchored on either bank of the river. Others use a floating cable attached to a single anchorage that may be on one bank or mid-channel. Where an overhead cable is used a "traveller" is usually installed on the cable and the ferry is attached to the traveller by a bridle cable. To operate the ferry either the bridle cable is adjusted or a rudder is used, causing the ferry to be angled into the current, and the force of the current moves the ferry across the river.

As the ferry cannot steer, a ramp is built at both ends and there is usually a set of controls facing in either direction.

Cable ferries are common where there is little other water-borne traffic that could get snagged in the cable or chains, where the water may be too shallow for other options, or where the river current is too strong to permit the safe crossing of a ferry not attached to the shore. Alignment of the platform at each end of the journey is automatic and, especially for vehicle ferries, safer than a free-moving ferry might be in bad conditions.

The castle above the campsite was the Everstein and was apparently Cinderella's house and hosts many Cinderella-related events throughout the year.

The campsite had a bar, which despite it being early evening seemed already to be full of drunk Germans.

We wanted to watch Tunisia vs. England in Group G so we moved on into town as the bar was full and it was still quite early. Bizarrely, heading into town we passed a display cabinet which contained model of Salisbury town centre complete with Decontamination Team.

We looked at a couple of places to eat, finally choosing one and eating schnitzel before returning to another aiming to watch the football 'with some atmosphere' as it was so described. It was empty apart from us. England only just managed to beat Tunisia 2-1 courtesy of two Harry Kane goals.

Distance cycled: 53km

Cumulative distance: 103km

Tuesday 19th June Polle to Hameln

(Bikeline Guide §12 to §17)

We were up by 07:00 and the ferry also noisily started at 07:00 so we got an early start. The route was along the B83 on the west (right) bank but before leaving we did manage to ask the ferryman why this ferry seemed to have an extra cable. He explained that a strong northerly (upstream) wind can have more effect on the ferry than the current, overcoming the 'reaction' by which the ferry is powered, so the extra cable is to counter this wind. You never stop learning!

Our destination for the night was 37km away in Hameln of pied piper fame. After about 3km we passed through the lovely town of Brevörde.

The route was all very flat and picturesque, arable farmland mostly. Rather uninhabited, so we were pleased to find a coffee stop – but it was shut till 14:00. The second we came to was shut until 14:30, the third until 11:00.

So we pressed on. After another 10km or so we took lunch at ANNA 19 in Pegestorf where asparagus was on offer.

Reaching Bodenwerder we had the option to cycle further north along the more main route along the B83 but we changed sides to the quieter route along the east bank.

Bodenwerder is known as the birthplace of Baron Münchhausen a fictional German nobleman created by the German writer Rudolf Erich Raspe in his 1785 book *Baron Munchausen's Narrative of his Marvellous Travels and Campaigns in Russia*. The character is loosely based on a real baron, Hieronymus Karl Friedrich, Freiherr von Münchhausen.

There are plenty of tourist attractions related to the good baron in Münchhausen Museum and in the old town and apparently (although we didn't visit) "pure fun on a fast-paced toboggan ride on the all-weather summer toboggan run in the middle of Münchhausen's Berggarten".

After about another 16km we indulged ourselves with a pointless but fun dogleg double ferry crossing firstly across the Alten Fährhaus then north along the B83 to have a look at Grohnde and back across the Weser on the Grohnder Fährhaus. Grohnde was a rather uninspiring town dominated by its nuclear power plant just to the north.

After another 14km or so we rolled into "rat-catcher town" Hameln.

The Pied Piper of Hamelin (German: *Rattenfänger von Hameln*, also known as the Pan Piper or the Rat-Catcher of Hamelin) is the titular character of a legend from the town of Hamelin (Hameln). The legend dates back to the Middle Ages, the earliest references describing a piper, dressed in multicoloured ("pied") clothing, who was a rat-catcher hired by the town to lure rats away with his magic pipe. When the citizens refused to pay for this service, he retaliated by using his instrument's magical power on their children, leading them away as he had the rats. This version of the story spread as folklore and has appeared in the writings of Johann Wolfgang von Goethe, the Brothers Grimm and Robert Browning, among others.

There are many contradictory theories about the Pied Piper. Some suggest he was a symbol of hope to the people of Hamelin, which had been attacked by plague; he drove the rats from Hamelin, saving the people from the epidemic.

The earliest known record of this story is from the town of Hamelin itself, depicted in a stained glass window created for the church of Hamelin, which dates to around 1300. Although the church was destroyed in 1660, several written accounts of the tale have survived.

The campsite at Hameln - Campingplatz Hameln an der Weser - on the river bank was unattractive and the pitches were unappealing, however, it did have incongruously luxurious showers, you'd think you were in an expensive spa hotel, except that they are free.

Hameln itself was a nice looking town with fine buildings, and was surprisingly quiet. The town was keen on its Pied Piper story, saying plenty about the rats, much less about the child abduction. We ate in a 'Mexican' place - Mexcalon on Osterstraße - and were seated in a remote and dark corner of the former bierkeller and former post office. The building was built in 1889 and the restaurant was in the old, brick, vaulted cellar. Mexcal is a mix of Mexican and Californian dishes. We were given a mountain of nachos and a long wait. By the time the main courses arrived we were somewhat jaded.

We slept well until a storm in the early hours.

Distance cycled: 37km

Cumulative distance: 140km

Wednesday 20th June Hameln to Bad Oeynhausen

(Bikeline Guide §17 to §21)

We were heading to Bad Oeynhausen for the evening. Setting off early, we left Hameln and set off on the east side of the river on roads parallel to the B83. We made good progress through more farmland, much of it given over to sugar-beet. After about 12km we reached Hessisch Oldendorf; another lovely, typical town of the area.

After another 4km or so as reached Großenwieden, another lovely town in the east bank of the Weser so of course we had to stop for coffee. Just after Großenwieden is of course Kleinenwieden where we came across a model planet Neptune. The associated information board had a map but unhelpfully it seemed to be inverted north-south, showing everything on the opposite bank to where we were. We had already missed Pluto but subsequently found Uranus, then Saturn albeit someone had stolen her rings.

This was a "Planet Path or Planetenweg", there are a couple of these on the Weser Radweg and many in Germany. The distance between the planets and information boards and the size of the "planets" are to scale. Unfortunately, in this case, the signs looked neglected. The remainder of the "Solar System" was within Rinteln. When we arrived at Rinteln Railway

Station to find out options for returning to Hamburg, the information available was disappointingly poor, considering we were in Germany. By way of compensation though, there were some little handmade 'funghi' on the grass.

Lunch on the other hand was excellent, and long, taken in the charming market square of Stadt Rinteln with its relaxing water feature and trolley-based decoration.

Rinteln was a mix of old i.e. Stadt Rinteln and new i.e. around the railway station. The fortified old part was lovely with narrow winding streets, picturesque corners and rows of 750 year old half-timbered houses. The former town hall dates from 1583 and most visible landmark is the tower of St. Nicholas built in 1238.

On the way out of Rinteln, we passed Doktorsee (doctor lake) an artificial swimming and leisure lake. The lake actually consists of two lakes that are separated from each other by a narrow headland, the smaller, western lake has direct access to the Weser.

The lake was created in the years up to 1960 through the mining of gravel and sand. After the mining stopped, the lake was used as a bathing lake. The name goes back to the meadows and pastures that were originally located here. These so-called "doctor pastures" were used by the professors of the University of Rinteln as pastures.

The route now had a long Westerly phase despite its overall northerly heading. We passed the spooky power station near Veltheim, a former coal-fired complex gradually closed down between 2000 and 2015.

En route we chatted to two binocular-equipped people about our respective holidays and about the birds we've all seen. They identified two of these as the Red Kite (der Rotmilan) and Grey Heron (der Graureiher).

We passed through Vlotho and continued towards Bad Oeynhausen. We had spent quite a lot of time discussing with some trepidation 'the lump', a topographical feature resembling a small hill, or spur, on the route map. Hitting the road at Mollbergen/Uffeln, we discovered the bike route had been amended to avoid the lump after all.

On the long 23km run into Bad Oeynhausen there was more than one campsite but we identified the correct one by the owner's name on the doorbell, Gerd Kütemeier. This was Campingplatz In Vössen, 32457 Porta Westfalica and was a great find. It was on the road called "In Vössen" just off the Radweg.

Herr Kütemeier turned out to be a retired farmer, our age, a nice chap and of a *very* cautious disposition: We could use a disposable barbecue but must ensure it is properly extinguished by immersion in the river. We must only put our tents where no other camper might drive over it (there was only one other camper). We must keep the facilities locked up at all times. We opted for a position tactically protected by trees and a picnic table, yet within emergency reach of the river. The site was picturesque with a long river frontage, but with quite a lot of traffic noise from a high road viaduct built in recent years which carried the main E30.

We were essentially camping in his back garden with the excellent facilities a separate (and only accessible from the exterior) part of his house.

We rode to the local supermarket, which did not sell disposable barbecues, so the risk of a campo inferno was somewhat reduced. But it certainly did have plenty of food, beer and wine, so we bought the lot.

Back at camp we met a new guest, a highly organised German woman, who was cycling to Rotterdam to see her grandchild. She declined a glass of wine, even though it must have been obvious to her how beneficial our regime was to us.

We spent the night around the tents eating and drinking our supplies and so early to bed.

Distance cycled: 50km

Cumulative distance: 190km

Thursday 21st June - staying in Bad Oeynhausen

(Bikeline Guide §21)

Logistically, we had to be in Hamburg the next day for our flight home. The best option for a train to Hamburg was from Minden, about 18km from our campsite, so rather than cycle further north then back again, we opted for a day's exploring the area and some general loafing. We often spend two nights in one place on our trips. Cycling is great of course but it's not always easy to see somewhere, when you're more passing through places and don't have time to look.

At 08:30 we looked out of the tents to find that it was raining so we went back inside. The granny on the other hand got up, cooked herself breakfast, struck camp and bravely cycled off towards Holland.

The rain eventually tailed off and all was lovely again, so we de-camped and headed into Bad Oeynhausen.

Bad Oeynhausen's main claim to fame is that it's a spa town and has the world's most highly carbonated thermal saltwater fountain, the *Jordansprudel*. On calm days the fountain gets up to 40m in height. The spring water is believed to have many medicinal qualities, giving rise to a number of health spas. We of course decided we had to sample some!

Also, Bad Oeynhausen is characterized by Gründerzeit buildings, a well-kept pedestrian zone with many cafes and shops and the spa gardens.

We pedalled into Bad Oeynhausen to the Bali Therme. According to their website, "Pure relaxation can be found in the Bali-Therme with the enchanting flair of the Indonesian island paradise in the middle of East Westphalia-Lippe". They also claim to "also do something for your fitness outside of the wet element" or that could just be my poor translation from the German. That's it we were hooked.

It was a great couple of hours bobbing around in the different inside and outside pools and having drinks in the café.

After our dip, we cycled through the Kurpark which had some lovely ornamental gardens and fountains, loafed, read our books and ate and drank.

A good day to recharge the batteries.

Distance cycled: 16km

Cumulative distance: 206km

Friday 22nd June Bad Oeynhausen to er... Hamburg Airport

We said goodbye to our campsite, the owner must have been very relieved that there had been no Major Incidents during our stay. We were due at Hamburg airport for an early evening flight to Bristol.

We were heading for about 18km mainly along the B61 to the larger city of Minden to catch a train to Hamburg.

We passed Porta Westfalica with its monumental Kaiser Wilhelm Monument (Kaiser-Wilhelm-Denkmal) clearly visible. The name "Porta Westfalica" is Latin and means "gate to Westphalia" as coming from the north, the gorge is the entry to the region of Westphalia.

Eventually we arrived in Minden and headed for the station Minden's claim to fame is apparently that it stands at the world's tallest waterway intersection, the Mittelland Canal crosses the Weser at a height of 13m.

Our train journey, largely a reversal of the outward one, was uneventful and the changes of train went smoothly.

The weather in Hamburg was benign as we reversed our route back to Hamburg City Bikes and retrieved our flight bags. We explained the pedal problem (and still had the old one) and they very kindly reimbursed us for the new set of pedals, excellent service!

Down the hill, on the waterfront was a transport interchange where buses and ferries met, we walked down there to a small outside bar for a couple of drinks prior to the final leg of the journey.

We pottered back to the airport via nearby Stadthausbrücke station and the train...everything was going absolutely swimmingly, nothing could possibly go wrong now!

Still, it was a bit odd that there was no one at the BMI check-in desk. Just a notice saying go to the information desk. Slowly it dawned that there was no flight, and no one from the airline to take any responsibility either. We didn't really know our rights at that point, which is a pity as seemingly we could have insisted on being returned to Bristol Airport at our airline's expense, however long and expensive the process. Instead of which we accept overnight accommodation in an airport hotel - the nearby Holiday Inn - and flights back to Heathrow next day. We were assured that we could reclaim onward travel to Bristol.

We learned subsequently (and not to our great surprise due to the very low passenger numbers) that BMI had gone bust so our claim for travel expenses from London to Bristol is still pending.

The free night was fine in the end, none of us had anything pressing to return for. We found our rooms, spread out our damp tents, used all the free toiletries in the shower and met downstairs for our free and not too bad meal. We were in the middle of a business park with nothing much else around so we stayed in the hotel bar for a couple of post meal drinks.

Distance cycled: 18km

Cumulative distance: 230km

23rd June - Hamburg Airport to Bristol

We were up early for a lovely free, all you can eat buffet, so we did eat all we could, it would have been rude not to!

A courtesy bus dropped us at the airport for our check in at the British Airways desk for our flight to Heathrow. We could have returned from Hamburg to Bristol courtesy of BMI via another airline but that would not have been for another couple of days so we opted for the earliest repatriation we could.

I was slightly apprehensive as the person who originally booked the BMI flight mistyped my surname as Adcick (the "I" and "O" are adjacent on the QWERTY keyboard). We had informed BMI prior to leaving Bristol, they would have charged to amend it but assured me it would be OK so we left it as was. There was nevertheless a nagging feeling that BA might pick up that the name on the ticket did not match my passport. My fears were unfounded and I boarded OK.

The rest of the trip was easy enough, an uneventful flight to Heathrow, a Heathrow Express train to London Paddington and a train home to Bristol.

BMI subsequently ignored all attempts by us to communicate with them about redress and ultimately went bust, leaving the appointed receivers to spend all the available money on themselves. We were only about £35 out of pocket in the end so not too bad.

Conclusion

This was another great trip. We were very fortunate to find Hamburg City Bikes who provided excellent service. The train journeys were easy and cheap and the connections were all smack on time. The campsites were also excellent, especially In Vössen.

The cycling was easy, possibly too easy as we were on the flat all the way and navigation was very straightforward.

Unlike many way marked routes i.e. canals and disused railways, we passed through places rather than past them so managed to see a good deal.

The countryside and towns were lovely but maybe too same old same old?

As usual it was good to spend two nights in one place having a mooch about and the spa was a great fund!

On the downside, it would have been good to have spent more time in Hamburg and BMI going belly up wasn't in the plan but it could have been worse, they could have gone bust BEFORE we went, every cloud!

Hopefully this has given the reader a flavour of what we did and might inspire you to do something similar.

Cycling in Germany - Why Do It?

Cycling in Germany is a pleasure. There are many cycle paths and way marked routes i.e. Radweg, many of which are river based. There are often signs between towns and villages marking the best route for cyclists.

German is larger than the UK and less populous so it's much less crowded, has fewer cars but fewer places of any size if you're looking for accommodation or somewhere to buy cake. The small roads i.e. local roads are very quiet and are perfect for cycling. German drivers are mostly tolerant of cyclists (cycling isn't such a huge deal as it is in neighbouring France, the French are extremely tolerant of cyclists).

Campsites in Germany are fewer than France but just as good. We booked all sites on our two camping trips and all accommodation on the Elbe trip. In France we tend to "wing it" more.

We ate well in Germany (a lot of pork based food and cabbage in the east) and of course the beer is superb!

As well as fantastic cycling infrastructure, the trains have great provision for carrying bikes on reliable, cheap, punctual and clean trains.

Everybody we met was interested in us and interesting to talk to, a very friendly nation.

What I do know for certain is that, if you've read this far you must have found something you liked so put the e-reader or book down now and start booking your trip.

About the author

For as long as I can remember I've cycled, to school, university (when it wasn't the trendy thing to do), places of work, nights out and more recently on holiday. Living in Bristol, despite the hills it's often the quickest and cheapest way to get around.

Following many years in IT, I left permanent employment in 2004 to enter the world of contract project management spending time labouring in the offices of many household names across the south west.

Turning 60 in 2017, I decided enough was enough and it was time to slow down, well, at least to try something new.

Following a chance meeting a few years ago (whilst cycling), I was asked if I'd like to train as a cycling instructor. After qualifying in October 2017 I've been working part time in schools and with adults on a 1 to 1 basis. It's quite a cool thing to tell people you're a "professional cyclist".

Other things that keep me busy are watching Southampton FC and Bristol Bears rugby, holidays, cycling, running and pub quizzes.

I live in Bristol with my teacher wife and three daughters in their 20s and I can be found on Facebook, Twitter and Instagram; peteradcockcycling.

Acknowledgements

My long suffering family allowing me the time and space to go and do this, they did have full access to the TV remote while I was away and apparently the "house was much tidier and quieter while you're were away" so that wasn't all bad.

My wife for proof reading, tactfully suggesting changes and helping me make sense of it all.

My daughters for helping me with the technical Instagram stuff.

Everybody we met be they cyclists, visitors or locals, who were, without exception charming, engaging, helpful, interested and interesting.

My fellow tourers who were very willing to let me loose on our trip notes (with a donation to future trip funds of course!).

Other titles by the same author

Cycling the Hebridean Way 10 islands, causeways and cake

Six days cycling across the Outer Hebrides, my first solo cycle tour and first cycle tour in the UK. Wonderful scenery, warm and welcoming people, plenty of cake, superb views, one hill, ferries, wildlife and beaches to die for. I scribbled some notes and have now got around to getting them into some sort of logical order. Go and do this, you don't have to be a hardened 100 mile a day cyclist, my biggest day was only 35 miles, be prepared for all weathers and I defy you not to have the best time.

Paperback edition: 138 pages; ISBN-10: 1655585959; ISBN-13: 978-1655585951; Dimensions: 15.2 x 0.9 x 22.9 cm

Kindle edition: File Size: 821KB; 109 pages; ASIN: B083GZRV32

***

Cycling Coast and Castles South - 2020: Cycling in a pandemic

2020 was the year of Covid, a pandemic which brought us lockdown. Foreign travel was next to impossible but in summer, the UK started to open up and we were encouraged to holiday at home. After a false start, I decided to cycle the spectacular Coast and Castles south from Tynemouth to Edinburgh. This took me through some of the north east's industrial heritage, I saw spectacular beaches, the glorious Tweed Valley, the damp Moorfoot hills and of course castles, lots of castles. Fuelled by coffee

and ice cream, this is my account of 5 superb days of cycling in this wonderful corner of our island.
Paperback edition: 145 pages, ISBN-13 : 979-

8688720792 **Kindle edition:** File Size: 5407KB; 147

pages; ASIN: B08JVFF1M4

***

So you want to go cycle touring? A beginner's guide.

Based on 20+ years of short tours (7 – 10 days), these are my thoughts on what you, as a beginner or novice (and maybe an experienced cycle tourer) might need to consider to get yourself on the road. I cover types of bike, whether or not to hire a bike, how to transport your bike to the start, where to stay, how to carry your stuff and what stuff to take. I also look at planning a trip, how fit you have to be (not very!) and what to eat and drink. Hopefully it will give you the push you need to dust off the bike and head off to see some of this wonderful world from the unique perspective which is from a bike saddle.

Paperback edition: 212 pages; ISBN-13: 979-8707078316; Dimensions: 15.24 x 1.22 x 22.86cm
Kindle edition: File Size: 11771KB; 147 pages; ASIN: B08X16HKC7

Cycle Commuting – A Beginner's Guide.

I retired from my previous work in 2017. Since then I've been teaching cycling skills and coaching on road 121 sessions with adults. Many of the concerns and worries are common and repeated so I've put the most common on paper which will hopefully help if you're thinking about commuting by cycle but not sure how to start. I've been commuting by cycle for 55 years to school, university and various places of work.

I cover reasons to commute by cycle, reasons not to and why these aren't insurmountable. Also what to wear, how to carry your stuff and which bike to use.

There are hints and tips on how to ride confidently and assertively on road based on my 121 work.

Paperback edition: 163 pages; ISBN-13 :979-8371729835, Dimensions : 15.24 x 0.94 x 22.86 cm

Kindle edition: ASIN :B0BRBK57GL, File size :6876 KB, 165 pages

☒☒☒

Cycling Lôn Las Cymru: Wales north to south
Opened in 1995, Lôn Las Cymru is one of the toughest of all long distance routes on the National Cycle Network (NCN). Sustrans describe it as a "challenge" route but it's short enough to be completed in a week by a self supported cyclist.
 With over 5,000m of climbing, the rider will need to be fairly fit and comfortable riding in often remote locations.
Lôn Las Cymru crosses three mountain ranges (Snowdonia, Cambrian Mountains and The Brecon Beacons) it is lumpy but the rewards are certainly worth it.
There are two finishing points, Cardiff which is all on

NCR 8 or Chepstow which requires a detour onto NCR 42 but does take the rider across the stunning Gospel Pass over the Black Mountains. Completed in July 2021 in the hottest week of the year, I decided to stick to NCR 8 and finish in Cardiff but I did consider the Chepstow finish as it would have been easy for me to cycle home to Bristol from there.

Paperback edition: 142 pages, ISBN-13: 979-8471944237

Kindle edition: File Size: 9582KB; 104 pages; ASIN: B09FK8S21M

***

Cycle touring in France and Germany: A selection of notes

For the last 9 years, 4 friends and I have made cycling expeditions to France and Germany and pottered along various cycle ways, rivers, canals, disused railways and small roads (apart from one mad cycle across Paris). During the trips we jotted down some notes which have languished on hard drives or on dusty sheets of paper. This is an attempt to pull them all together, add some more information and publish in the hope they may be useful to others considering similar trips. The adventures were: France: 2012: The river Loire - Nevers to Angers; 2014: La Rochelle to Bordeaux; 2015: Circular expedition east of Bordeaux; 2016: Bordeaux – Cognac – Bordeaux; 2017: St Malo - Rennes - St Malo; 2019: Montpellier and Germany; 2011: Cycling the Elbe; 2013: Cycling the Black Forest Cycle Way; 2018: Cycling the Weser-

Radweg - Hann. Münden to Minden. Don't expect 100s of km a day, more relaxed journey looking at interesting places and sampling the local delicacies.

Paperback edition: 340 pages; ISBN-13: 979-8635586709; ASIN: B086Y3S9GB; Product Dimensions: 15.2 x 2.2 x 22.9 cm

Kindle edition: File Size: 983KB; 215 pages; ASIN: B086XDGL8J

***

Cycle touring in France: A selection of notes

A collection of notes (with enhancements) from 6 cycle tours in France in the areas of Bordeaux, La Rochelle, St Malo, Rennes, the Loire valley and Montpellier. Tales of 5 friends pottering from 0 km to 50 km a day depending on how we felt. A good mix of hiring bikes, taking our own bikes and camping. Hopefully some of these trips may inspire the reader to attempt something similar.

Paperback edition: 217 pages; ISBN-13; 979-8633995602; ASIN: B086PPJHVN; Dimensions: 15.2 x 1.4 x 22.9 cm

Kindle edition: File Size; 987KB; 151 pages; ASIN: B086RS9L2W

***

Cycling around Bordeaux - Three Routes in Western France

An account of 5 intrepid souls and 3 cycling trips in the Bordeaux area of western France. Firstly, La Rochelle to Bordeaux, secondly a loop from Bordeaux using part of the Roger Lapébie cycle path and thirdly a loop from Bordeaux to Cognac returning to Bordeaux. An adventure in the sun, getting lost, fearing kidnap, pleasant cycling, wine, cheese and putting the world to rights.

Kindle edition: File Size: 898KB; 63 pages; ASIN: B085VFZ38Q

***

Cycling the Black Forest Cycle Way (Südschwarzwald-Radweg): Adventures in three countries - 2013

A cycling tour of the southern Black Forest cycle way (the Südschwarzwald-Radweg) from Frieburg to Basel, a detour into France and back to Freiburg. A story of wonderful scenery, lovely people, border crossings and unnecessarily transporting a pineapple.

Kindle edition: File Size: 797KB; 32 pages; ASIN: B086417J9F

***

The river Loire - Nevers to Angers, châteaux and cheese

In 2012 it was decided 5 of us would celebrate our friend's looming 60th birthday by undertaking a long distance cycle ride - slowly! This is a tale of cycling the western part of the Loire valley i.e. the flat bit, more chateaux then you can shake a baguette at, wine, cheese and camping on islands in the stream.

Kindle edition: File Size: 850KB; 45 pages; ASIN: B085VHX1LD

***

Cycling in Brittany - a short trip from St Malo to Rennes - 2017

A short trip cycling from St Malo, west along the coast via Dinard, then south to Rennes via Dinan along a Voie Vert. A train ride north from Rennes and a gentle cycle west to St Malo. An easy trip to do in a few days with plenty of options to detour. Some of it could be done in a long weekend.

Kindle edition: File Size: 886KB; 37 pages; ASIN: B086N3PD6M

***

Cycling around Montpellier - Coping with the heat - 2019

A trip to and from Montpellier in southern France. Our original plan was curtailed due to record breaking temperatures of over 40C. Not a huge amount of cycling but much swimming in the sea and campsite pools but these notes give the reader a flavour of possible routes around this area.

Kindle edition: File Size: 996KB; 30 pages; ASIN: B086RQK9SR

***

Cycling the Weser-Radweg : Hann. Münden to Minden - 2018

A 220km ride along part of the river Weser cycle way (Weser Radweg) from Hann. Munden to Mindon via Hamburg. Lovely flat cycling, some beautiful villages, great camp sites and plenty of beer.

Kindle edition: File Size: 953KB; 30 pages; ASIN: B086RW6PXB

***

Cycling the Elbe Cycle Route (Elberadweg) : Lutherstadt Wittenberg to the Czech border - 2011

A trip along 220km of the Elbe cycle way to the Czech border via Berlin. Much beer to drink and wonderful cycling. Considering this was our first experience of taking bikes on a plane, it all went very well.

Kindle edition: File Size: 671KB; 33 pages; ASIN: B086SDCSFR

Printed in Dunstable, United Kingdom